I0469893

Dancing into the Unknown

Osho Painting & Art Therapy

by
Meera Hashimoto

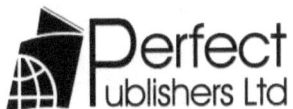

Copyright © Meera Art Foundation 2017

All rights reserved. No part of this publication may be reproduced, stored in a retrieval system or transmitted in any form or by any means, electronic, mechanical, audio, visual or otherwise, without prior written permission of the copyright owner. Nor can it be circulated in any form of binding or cover other than that in which it is published and without similar conditions including this condition being imposed on the subsequent purchaser.

www.meera-art-foundation.com

Consultant Editor: Subhuti
Editor for Intro and Appendix: Punya
Cover Design: Hamido Frank Kardell
Photo of Author: Maggie Zhao
Paintings on Cover: Meera Hashimoto

OSHO® is a registered
Trademark of Osho International Foundation ("OIF")

Quote by Osho © Osho International Foundation

PERFECT PUBLISHERS LTD
23 Maitland Avenue
Cambridge
CB4 1TA
England
www.perfectpublishers.co.uk

Whether you are creating something...
all that has to be remembered is that it is coming out of a
silence within you,
that it has a spontaneity.
It is not prearranged, pre-programmed, pre-thought.
As you are creating something you go on being surprised
yourself –
you have left yourself in the hands of existence.
Osho

Contents

Foreword

by Svagito

I am pleased to publish Meera's last book, just a year after she left her body. She died unexpectedly in an accident that shocked everyone. The way she left was certainly her style of doing things. Not that she had decided to depart from this world at that moment, but her way of leaving seems to be so much in tune with her way of living: with totality, with a readiness to let go each moment, with spontaneity, doing things without regret – and always to the surprise of everyone.

Of course, I wished she would have stayed around a bit longer to add more colours to the painting of her extraordinary life. Maybe she would have added a few more chapters to this book or changed a few lines here and there. Nobody knows for sure whether the book is finished or not; maybe it was indeed still a work in progress, but I feel that everything she wanted to share should now be made available.

I remember that in a workshop Meera once mentioned an English poet who was famous for never finishing his poems. When this was addressed to him, he had answered, "Anyone who reads my poems can finish them himself!" After telling this story to her audience, Meera added with a big smile, "I like that!" Maybe this is what we can also do: continue Meera's work and let her vision of creativity grow, expand and reach new heights.

In this book, Meera presents a new vision of art therapy; the Osho Art Therapy that she developed according to Osho's vision. Unlike in common art therapy, it does not reduce painting to a mere method to help us overcome traumas or psychological problems.

Painting can do much more, if our expression comes from a space of meditation and silence within. It can help us connect with something that is beyond mind and take us to a higher state of consciousness.

Meera was a master in awakening the mysterious, the spontaneous and illogical in people. In her courses she continuously created situations so that her participants could awaken to their own creative intelligence and re-discover their hidden treasure. I hope that this book will be an inspiration to start, or continue, the journey of self-discovery through painting.

The manuscript that Meera left behind had been worked on, together with Subhuti, for one and a half years, the text based on their many talks. It had no title, nor a clear ending. I decided to publish it the way she left it, but I chose the title and subtitle.

Because this second book is exclusively about art therapy – also her last DVDs are on this topic – I chose 'Osho Art Therapy' as subtitle. And the main title, 'Dancing into the Unknown' came up while reading the text and remembering some of her last words before she herself disappeared into the unknown. I truly believe she left this world *dancingly*.

I have also asked Meera's long-time assistants to write a few reflections about their experiences of working with her and used it as an epilogue. On the one hand it is an ending to the book and on the other it is a new beginning; it is now up to them to carry the flame that was ignited in them through Meera's fire and passion.

I would like to conclude with Meera's own words that show her love and passion for painting and for people's inner growth:

"I feel that everything I received from Osho is coming closer and closer to my expression in the paintings I create. It is painting without effort...

"It's not dead. It's alive, throbbing with energy and life. I'm so excited that sometimes I can't sleep because I want to get up early in the morning and paint. Each day is filled with a sense of newness. Each day I'm intrigued by the discoveries I make as I throw myself into the unknown...

"Paintings coming out of this approach are a surprise to my own eyes, and I want to bow down to every new painting that is born in front of me. In such moments, I feel the significance of being alive, and if I can share this thrill with others, so they can make their own unique footprint on this earth, giving birth to their own creativity, then I am most happy."

From *ReAwakening of Art* by Meera

Acknowledgements

After long years of searching for a definition of Osho Art Therapy, I have come to a certain clarity that was missing before. Even though I present many different elements in this book, I can now offer them to you in the spirit of oneness, bringing all my ideas and experiences about therapy together and giving them expression as a single voice.

This book is dedicated to Osho and his entire work, because it is my sincere wish to be able, in some way, to help transmit his immensely valuable gift to the coming humanity. Since I was living in the presence of the Master for more than a decade, I feel the need to write this book in homage and gratitude for what I have gained.

Almost 30 years have passed and yet, sitting in meditation, listening to Osho's voice on any of his recorded discourses, I feel his message is being freshly delivered, in this moment, as if it is happening right now.

Some people are surprised, even shocked, when I tell them, "It's good he left his body when he did, because that enabled me to understand that each of his sannyasins is a living message. It's up to us how we develop his vision."

I remember him once saying, "My work is done, but people will continue to connect with me if their hearts are open. They will make my vision more varied, more colourful, more profound, because human consciousness is continually growing, becoming better and better each moment...."

It is an amazing statement. Unlike the founders of conventional religions, he is not declaring that there is nobody better than him, but recognising that the song of humanity will go on rising to higher and higher peaks of consciousness.

I wish to bring Osho's message into the market place, addressing those who are in the helping professions, those who are working with people, using the three elements of Art, Therapy and Meditation. I want to make it simple, so that this book can be used as a manual when working with others.

As I write these words, the faces of participants in my trainings around the world pass before my mind's eye, including those in India, Japan, Malaysia, Spain, England, Ireland, Germany, Italy, Greece, Sweden, Norway, Finland, Taiwan, Mexico, Brazil...all those beautiful people who have ventured into my world. I dedicate my book to them, as well as to my Master.

I acknowledge my beautiful partner, Svagito, whose love for people's growth is so immense. Over the years, I have been present in his workshops and trainings, and I bow down to his passion for therapy, passing onto others the keys to healing and happiness.

I thank Sagarpriya, whose love for Osho and his work is absolute, and who taught me so much. Thanks also to the therapists and dancers who have brought me the joy of expressing myself through dance, including Viram, Navanita, Chetan, Niketan, Kantomoe, Birgitta, Soohee and Amiyo. And to the musicians who played in our workshops, or whose albums I have enjoyed sharing through my work, such as Karunesh, Devakant, Vikram, Almasta, Milarepa, Miten, Premal, Hariprasad, René Aubry, Amar, Joshua, Rishi, Bhavia Arjun and many more.

Special thanks to Bert Hellinger for giving us the gift of Family Constellation Therapy, and to other therapists who have taught me, such as Prasad, Prabodhi and Premananda – I have already mentioned Sagarpriya and Svagito.

My gratitude is extended, of course, to my family. To my father, who allowed me to study art and inspired me to go abroad to explore my creativity. To my mother whose love and trust was immense. A haiku poet of distinction, she taught me how to live in tune with nature and to trust what life brings.

To my friends who support me and love me: Gatasansa, Lashimi, Vayu, Bhaven, Abhinava, Henna, CD, Manav, Ojas, Satyanand, Prageeta, Neeten, Amalurras, Premendra.

To dear Subhuti, my editor and co-writer, who made it possible for me to publish this book. I love his way of giving a smooth flow to the words that pour out of me. It is fun to work with him and I notice the fire of my inspiration burns brighter when he is looking over my shoulder.

To Hamido, my beloved cameraman, who has been filming and documenting my workshops, trainings and paintings for over 20 years. Osho once told him to make his home a meditation centre and in a way, he is still doing it – so many people are being helped and supported by him.

I wish to acknowledge Jayesh, Neelam, Amrito, Garimo, Pramod, Raj, Dhyanesh and all those who have done their best to maintain and improve the Pune ashram after Osho left his body, keeping the place open so that people from all over the world can come and experience meditation.

It is my personal understanding that one needs the company of other, like-minded people on the spiritual journey in order to see oneself reflected in the eyes of other meditators and, in this way, become mature. The ashram, which is now called Osho International Meditation Resort, is an oasis created for this purpose.

I have respect and gratitude towards those who keep the Resort together.

Thanks also to those who have made Osho's message freely available on the Internet, because now Osho's message can be heard, read and seen in any country, at any time, in any corner of the planet.

We who are inspired by Osho's vision do not need to know each other directly, but together our energy and creativity can light a fire in people's hearts and transform mundane lifestyles into explosions of vitality and colour.

Introduction

I want to begin by giving a little background to my work, showing how my interest in Osho Art Therapy was born.

In 1974, I was living by myself as an artist in Spain and was not even aware of the need for a spiritual dimension in my life. A new adventure began during a trip to India, when I met Osho at his ashram in Pune and was captivated by his charisma, his energy, his vision of life and his strange but effective methods of meditation.

Osho appealed to me because he never interfered in people's lives. He never told them what was right and wrong. He simply encouraged us to explore how to be authentic individuals, using the awareness gained through meditation to guide one's own actions.

Naturally, when he asked me what I want to do in Pune, I told him, "I want to paint." He simply said "Good!" He was attracting all kinds of people – musicians, artists, therapists, teachers, writers, actors – and somehow, even though Osho's ashram was small and crowded, there was space for all of us.

In the morning, when he was giving discourse, about 3000 people were sitting, meditating and listening at the same time, soaking up the energy like so many thirsty sponges. You can imagine how alive the atmosphere was in that little ashram.

Around that time, Osho was giving 'darshan' every evening, meeting personally with disciples and visitors, welcoming newcomers and often suggesting certain groups for people. It was a hot, passionate era. All kinds of psychotherapists from all over the world were gathering around Osho. It was a Mecca of therapy and the therapists, too, were learning, adding the dimension of meditation to their work.

Darshan was a direct and intriguing process. The group leaders would sit together with their participants and Osho would ask them, one by one, "How was it for you?" It was so intimate and powerful to be there.

I decided to quit Spain completely and live in Osho's Pune ashram, because I sensed there was another way to live, as part of a spiritual community rather than as a separate entity. That was the time – it must have been 1979 – when Osho suggested that I create an Art Group.

Naturally, when you form an art group, you meet all kinds of artists and art lovers, and soon we were busy sharing our ideas about how the art group should function. Everybody's inner longings and standpoints about art were being discussed and examined.

We were given a space in a lush green compound, next to the weaving department. I will never forget the first time I stepped into that compound. I felt like Alice entering Wonderland. The sound of the weaving looms was like music and the light filtering through the trees, bushes and lattice-like walls created an effect like stained-glass windows in a church.

Parmita, a young American woman in charge of the weaving, gave me some practical advice from her own experience: "If you want to make your Art Group happen, you have to live here."

So, I did, nervously at first, because I was used to living in a house and this seemed like outdoor living, in a structure made very simply from bamboo and plywood. All I really needed was a mattress and a mosquito net.

From my days as an art student in Tokyo, when I was teaching children to paint as a part-time job, I intuitively understood that painting must be done on the floor, not standing like European artists. This way, your body is involved and painting becomes a dance.

Those children taught me many things about simplicity and creativity. For example, one small boy was crying and when I asked him to tell me his problem, he replied, "I can't paint if there is no object in front of me to copy."

It started me thinking. It made me wonder: where has the innocence and natural, spontaneous, expression of our creativity gone? How did this boy lose it? How can I help him get it back?

Playfulness was an important key to the solution. I remember Osho once saying, "What is the difference between painting and cleaning? Painting, you throw colours on a canvas. Cleaning you throw water on the floor and...look! You have done an invisible painting!"

This approach took the seriousness out of painting for me and from then on, I always tried to include playfulness and joy as basic qualities of the art group.

Another key that came to us from Osho was his insistence that spiritual growth requires us to dive into the unknown. Nothing can happen while we stick to what we know. This idea appealed to us, because many of us had never painted like that. Up to this point, a painting project had to be born out of an idea, an initial concept, which preceded it. Moving directly into painting made our creations unique and fresh.

I also realised that one doesn't need special talent for painting. This creative impulse is hidden in us all. This led me to invite therapists of all kinds to come and work with our group, because I was exploring the reasons why creative energy had been blocked and how to release it, whether through remembering our childhood issues and what our parents said to us, or through bodywork, breath work, dance and meditation.

Seen from this perspective, the world of therapy is rich, offering many different pathways to higher consciousness and, in this book, you will come to meet some of the therapeutic methods I have integrated into my work.

When Osho left Pune for the United States in 1981, our Art Group also started travelling We staged an exhibition of our paintings in Mumbai, we formed a rural community deep in the mountains in Sicily and we moved onto a houseboat in Amsterdam. We had no money, but always, somehow, through our longing and passion for art, we survived and prospered through many adventures.

This is what I invite my participants to explore with me in my workshops and trainings: connecting with the fire of our passion for life and reclaiming our dignity as naturally creative beings.

It is within reach of everyone. It is our birth right.

Chapter One

Art, Therapy & Meditation

It's a challenge to be human. It's a challenge to live your life to the max, to explore and discover all the different dimensions of your own being.

This book is part of the challenge. It's an opportunity for people who want to explore art, therapy and meditation together, for people who are looking for their true identity through these three avenues.

My approach is essential and immediate. It's not a gradual, systematic method. Either you transform yourself in this moment, or you don't. And it's always your choice, your freedom, to allow it, to encourage it, or prevent it.

Most conventional methods of art therapy rely on an analytical approach. But the problem is that the more you analyse yourself, the more you move into the structure of the mind – and the mind has no exit, no way to get you out of the limitations imposed by your own personality.

With the essential, with the immediate, there's a better chance for people to re-experience their original self, hidden deep inside, which is your child-like spirit. This spirit never dies and is innocent. We are trained to forget our innocence, but it is always there, waiting for us to rediscover it.

As soon as we were born, we were subjected to a process of education, which can also be called conditioning, or social training. We were taught how to behave, what to say, what to believe...and so on. During this process, we developed fixed ideas about ourselves. This is how the mind is created.

The work of a spiritual mystic like Osho is to help us cut through this conditioning to reclaim our true identity as individuals. Meditation and therapy are used to recognise how our energy has been blocked, to understand what ideas and beliefs prevent us from saying a wholehearted 'yes' to life – 'yes' to that exuberant space inside, which never dies.

To separate oneself from one's true nature is to separate oneself from existence, from the Whole, and this is the root cause of suffering. Unfortunately, this happens to all of us. It's not our fault. It's the product of our upbringing. However, the good news is: we can do something about it. We can undo the damage. If you look at yourself from this angle, you will drop the struggle created by the gap between your personality and your spontaneous nature. You will understand that healing is possible when you disappear as a personality, as a separate ego, and allow yourself to be a part of the Whole.

The problem is not a big one. How can it be? We are so small, compared with this vast existence surrounding us. So, the problem must likewise be small. If you adopt this way of looking at your 'problem', the work is almost done. Then you can look at it with humour, understanding and detachment. The problem is there, but your relationship with it changes.

My work is to bring Osho's approach into the world of visual art, reclaiming the innocence and creativity with which we came into this world. Like I say, it is a challenge. If I teach art directly, showing people standard techniques of how to paint, I am repeating the tendency of all childhood education – imposing something from outside.

Instead, I put the spotlight on the inside, looking at what is already there. I shine light into the dark corners of the human psyche which are obstructing our energy flow and our ability to say 'yes' to life.

2

It's like taking weeds out of a garden. When the soil is free and healthy, the roses grow naturally and bloom by themselves, radiating colour and showering their fragrance. Borrowing Osho's words: "Blossoming is our very nature, you simply need to prepare the ground."

This training is called Osho Art Therapist Training. The focus is on you, on bringing awareness to the source from which your actions arise. This is the whole point. If your action arises out of a conscious state then whatever you say, or do, or paint, is going to be right. But if your action is mechanical, learned, unconscious, then, even if you are a technically skilled artist, the action will be wrong and your painting will lack vitality.

From my side, I offer two avenues in a training:

1) The process of taking back your personal creativity.
2) Understanding the approach required when working with a group of people around the issue of creativity.

In both cases it's you and your motivation that matters.

Three Types of People

I have many kinds of students, from many different countries. They can be broadly categorised into three groups:

1) People in helping professions who work with people, including therapists, art therapists, consultants and teachers. Usually, they are suffering symptoms of burn-out. They have lost the motivation to work in a fresh, vital and exciting way.

2) Artists, including well-established artists, who feel they have lost contact with their original creative expression.

3) Anyone who understands that somehow their creative impulse has been blocked. They know they are carrying negative beliefs about themselves, such as: "I have no artistic talent, I can't paint, I wasn't born to be a creator, I was born with two left hands."

All of these people become healthier through Osho's approach, because whatever we think we have lost is really still inside us. We didn't lose it. We just forgot it.

Osho reminds us that we are Buddhas. By our very nature, we are fulfilled, creative, harmonious beings. We are already at home in ourselves. All that is needed is to say 'yes' to this essential state.

It sounds easy, but, of course, it is not. The obvious is the most difficult. The immediate looks farthest away. Seeing is easy, but how to reach there? The answer given by so many spiritual teachers down through the centuries is, of course, 'meditation'. Meditation is the key, the door, the method.

Today, we have another avenue available as a complement to meditation: Western psychological methods of therapy. I refer to therapy that is used not as a way of treating illness, but as a way of acquiring more health, raising self-awareness; therapy that helps us to look inside, to pass through the barriers and blocks, clearing an inner space for meditation.

In my work, I use Star Sapphire and Family Constellation as my main therapeutic tools for self-discovery. First, I want to focus on Star Sapphire.

Star Sapphire

Star Sapphire therapy was developed by a colleague of mine, Sagarpriya DeLong Miller. She works with the understanding – first noted by Carl Gustav Jung – that there are two sides to our psychology: a masculine side and a feminine side.

If you study painting, you can see that all the best works have these two qualities: masculine and feminine. If one quality is ignored or missing, the artist's expression will be poor and flat. It won't carry the fragrance of mystery, which manifests through complementary contradictions – opposite qualities existing together without conflict or compromise.

A person who wants to learn artistic expression needs to ask, "What is painting?" And to answer this question, he must go deeper into himself and ask, "Who am I? What is the significance of *my* existence? What does it mean to be really human?"

One answer to this kind of self-inquiry is to balance the male and female polarities inside ourselves, but I don't mean 'balance' in the normal sense of finding a middle point between them. Osho's definition of balance is different. According to him, balance happens when two apparent opposites disappear in one harmonious dance.

That's what I teach people who come to me: to disappear into the painting.

Family Constellation

Family Constellation, developed by Bert Hellinger, offers an opportunity to discover the burdens that children unintentionally take on, at an early age, from members of previous generations in their families.

Hellinger's work is awe-inspiring. He has discovered that if somebody was not acknowledged, or was pushed out of the family, then a later family member will, without knowing it, be compelled to represent this person. A child who may never have met the forgotten ancestor will be forced to live out this character in some way – by becoming sick, taking on misery, or suffering, and so on.

Beneath the surface of Hellinger's work lies the need for every family member to be loved and respected. For example, even if one person was missing in my family line, I would not be here. This understanding can be beneficial, because ultimately you need to include everyone and everything in your ancestry, even going back to nature, to the fish, to the animals. With this insight you become humble, understanding and respectful.

In my work, I focus mainly on the dynamic between parents and children. Hellinger identifies two movements: one is that you need to come close to your parents, as a child; the other is that you need to move away from them as a natural part of growing up.

In most people, neither movement is complete. Many people are fighting with their parents, many people feel no gratitude for being born, for being raised. Hellinger teaches us that you can't really separate from your parents unless you first bow down to them and thank them for all they have done for you. Only then can you be free to be yourself.

Of course, this shows up in people's paintings. Many times, after a Family Constellation session, I see dramatic changes in a person's style, approach, freedom of expression. The energy that has been chained up is suddenly free to dance with the colours on the canvas.

The Body Comes First

Another important aspect of Osho's vision that I use in my trainings is the understanding that the body comes first. The body is the most innocent part of our existence, unlike our busy, chattering minds, which often ignore what the body tries to tell us.

We are strangers to our own bodies. Just recently, I was listening to an Osho discourse where he was saying that if you cut off the heads of people, even a wife and a husband won't be able to recognise their partners.

So, this is a foundation of Osho's work: to come back to our body, to say 'yes' to our body, to make more roots in our body. When we do this, we also become more open to the present moment. The mind mainly lives in past and future, but the body is always here and now.

I work a lot with body awareness. I come from Japan, where there are many traditions that focus on the feet. For example, Gautam Buddha's Vipassana meditation has a walking stage in which one's awareness is focused on the sensation of the feet touching the ground.

In the 'No' dance school, all emphasis is placed on the feet and back. My dance teacher used to say to me, "When your back is absolutely present, then you become a dancer."

Saying 'yes' to the body, means saying 'yes' to ourselves. But unfortunately, we don't say 'yes'. Instead, we hide our nakedness. We have forgotten the grandeur of living naturally, like animals. The face is our only identity and yet, when you look at people's faces, they are so stiff, almost frozen. They don't move. They don't change expression.

It's as if we have a fixed image of ourselves and don't want to risk going beyond the facade we present to the world around us.

In my workshops, I work a lot with freeing the muscles of the face, because we accumulate so much tension in this part of our body.

Emotional Expression

Next, comes an awareness of our emotions and the need to express them. Osho's method of Dynamic Meditation is the best example of how this can be done, because it uses vigorous breathing to wake up our energy, bypass the mind and connect with our emotions. Through fast, deep, chaotic breathing, we go into a space where the mind can't maintain control. This, in turn, allows us to enter into feelings and express them.

You may have noticed that in normal daily life the mind is very busy trying to keep our emotions under control. We are afraid of expressing ourselves and afraid of others doing the same. It's a social taboo. Women are allowed to cry while watching sad movies, men are allowed to get excited and shout at football matches, and that's about it.

With awareness, we can connect with our emotions and release them, giving them expression. This is essential on the spiritual path, because energy needs to move if it is to remain alive and vibrant. Whatever we hold back and keep bottled up inside us becomes poison.

In my understanding of Osho's approach to meditation, unless you can release your emotions, silence will never come to you. You may go to the Himalayas and pretend to sit silently, but inside you will be sitting in a volcano of blocked energy. In short, my work is to help people understand what hinders them from enjoying life, what prevents them from singing a song of nature – singing the song they already have inside themselves, thereby making life more rich and meaningful.

Painting as a Mirror

There are many kinds of therapy, but painting is unique in the way it reflects you. When you paint, you see yourself mirrored on the paper in front of you. When you stop and see what you've done, you *have* to face your own reflection. Then you have a choice: either you throw it in the garbage, so you don't need to acknowledge it, or you look at yourself and accept it.

Picturesque expression is non-verbal and connects directly with the unconscious part of our minds, so the intellectual and rational part cannot interfere. That's why you can be *so* surprised at what comes out during a painting session – both good and bad. In a very short time, this work helps people to understand what is happening in their psyche.

This is the purpose of my book. I want to give a hand, helping people open up to everything, both inside and outside, because life can be so rich, so beautiful, and can offer so much opportunity to grow.

I hear many comments, from all over the world, about the effectiveness of this work. I meet people after fifteen years, who tell me how much they gained from one group. Even if they didn't fully understand it at the time, even if the insights took time to mature – like learning the art of letting go, for example – it gave them a hint, an indication, of what life can be like.

A whole and healthy life, as I said in the beginning, is an expression of true balance. That's what my painting workshops are all about.

Chapter Two

Primal Painting

Primal Painting is the backbone of my teaching. Childhood issues, which are always connected to the relationship with one's parents, are touched in almost all my workshops and trainings. In Primal Painting, we make it the main focus, taking a long, deep look at attitudes and feelings that we've kept locked away inside ourselves since we were very young.

Everybody carries beliefs about themselves that were formed during those primal years, including all kinds of notions about one's own creative abilities. Unfortunately, these beliefs are usually negative. It's interesting for me to see that even therapists who have worked on childhood issues can easily say to me, "Painting? It's not for me. I have two left hands!" Meaning, of course, they have no talent.

So, our method is: look within ourselves and see how such beliefs were adopted in the first place.

Natural Creative Ability

When I look at small children, under the age of three, they never question their creative abilities. If the materials are given – crayons, paints, charcoal – they just use them, following their curiosity and natural sense of playful adventure.

For example, I used to take care of my sister's child when she was two years old. One day, as an experiment, I gave her several big pots of colours, big brushes and many papers, without any instruction.

I didn't say, "Now paint a house," or "Now paint a tree." I just left her alone to do whatever she wished. She stayed there for hours, continuously inventing new ways to paint on different papers.

That's when I understood it's not right for adults to say things like, "I have no talent." It's pure nonsense. Of course, not everyone can be a Picasso or a van Gogh, but everyone can access their natural sources of creative energy. It's our birth right. It's a gift from the generosity of existence.

When I offer a course in Art Therapy, it is different from a regular painting training, in which I am basically teaching people how to make good paintings. From the therapeutic perspective, painting is more like a mirror, expressing yourself in order to see your attitudes, beliefs and fears reflected on the paper in front of you.

It is well known that pictures connect with a deeper level of the human mind than thinking and intellectual ideas. Hence, the real power of television and movies to impact an audience lies in the visual images they use rather than their words. So, when we begin to paint, we easily access unconscious layers of the mind that will influence the way we express ourselves.

For example, some people, when they begin to paint, quickly become attached to certain aspects of painting – they like certain colours, lines, shapes. Then it becomes difficult for them to move, or change. They may not be satisfied with what they have done, and they may feel the limitations they have imposed on themselves, but they want to keep it like that. Why? Because they carry so much fear about meeting the unknown, letting go of the familiar – they cling to what they know. They are reluctant to risk.

When this happens, it's a great opportunity for people to examine their patterns and conditioning.

If they can drop their conditioning and open to a bigger understanding of life, they will have a different attitude towards painting and, naturally, this will be reflected in what they create.

So, let me repeat: in Art Therapy, we are not teaching people to make a good painting. Rather, painting is used as a mirror to see our conditionings, beliefs and fears reflected on the paper in front of us.

No Fixed Ideas

I invited another small child – he was about three years old – into one of my painting workshops in Denmark, and he remained intrigued by the play of colours on paper for hours.

I was watching him carefully to see how he managed it. And it was so simple. He was effortlessly bringing his energy and his awareness into the present moment, here and now, opening himself to life. When you do this, the present moment becomes magical. And that's all I'm teaching in my workshops. That's what Primal Painting is about.

Watching him, I had another insight. He would paint in a certain way until he became bored with it, then he would completely change the painting – by splashing bright pink on grey, for example – or pick up a new piece of paper and begin afresh.

He had no concept, no fixed idea, about creating 'a painting'; he had no attachment to what he was doing, so for him there was no difficulty in self-expression. By observing him, I came to understand that any problem that pops up while we are painting must be associated with some concept or attitude we have already acquired. So, as we paint, we continually witness our own state of mind manifesting before us on the paper.

For example, when we sit down in front of a clean piece of paper, with paints by our side, we normally have the intention to create something particular. Perhaps we already know that it's going to be: a seascape, a landscape, a still life. As our idea takes shape, we become attached to what we are painting, or, alternatively, frustrated by the fact that it's not turning out the way we want. Within a very short time, we find ourselves confined by our own concepts about what we should, or should not, be doing.

So, the first thing I teach in Primal Painting is: "Forget that it's a painting."

As soon as you think, "Now I am going to paint," all kinds of judgements and beliefs flood the mind: what is beautiful, what is ugly, what is right, what is wrong. All of these notions conspire to block your spontaneity.

When Your Creativity was Blocked

One of my first tasks in Primal Painting is to guide people back in time to one of those childhood moments when creativity was blocked. I begin by inviting them to sit in front of a blank sheet of white paper and pay attention to what memories and feelings are triggered by this simple act.

"Maybe you wanted to impress somebody – your teacher, your mother – and you couldn't manage it." I suggest, "Maybe you painted a picture and one of your parents expressed disappointment. Maybe somebody told you, 'Don't paint this way...that's not right!' Maybe you were pushed and hurried and told, 'Get on with it!'"

"One way or another, you got the message to be somebody else rather than who you are, and in order to be loved, to be accepted, you trimmed and adjusted your creative energy to match the expectations of others," I continue.

13

"Slowly, these restrictive patterns became an ingrained habit in all aspects of life. Whatever the activity – relating, working, dancing, or talking – the same negative attitudes were repeated."

Uncovering Memories

It's time to make an investigation. I instruct the participants to close their eyes and invite them to become a small child again. Then I ask, "What is this child's intention? What does he really want to express? And why? Is it to gain attention or approval? Is this approval from your mother, or your father?"

It's my aim to uncover those memories where shock occurred, because this is one of the keys to undoing the damage. Once you start remembering, once you consciously re-live a traumatic experience with the wisdom and compassion of an adult, healing starts to happen. The blocked creativity begins to flow again.

There are many methods for connecting with one's inner child. For example, sometimes I invite people to sit with eyes closed, hands resting on their thighs, in an open position, with both palms facing upwards. Then I guide them into an exploration, saying, "Imagine that in your right palm sits the child who got hurt, shocked and criticised. She sits there with all kinds of powerful emotions and hurt feelings. Take time to acknowledge and welcome this child as she is. Make sure to remember her age, her intention, her energy, what she was doing when she experienced this shocking intervention by her parents or some other authority figure. Look in her eyes, talk to her, listen to her…"

Opening a possibility for the child to express herself, the gestalt begins to change. Instead of being struck dumb, incapable of response, the child starts to share what really happened and how she felt. In this way, her authentic energy – suppressed or distorted at the time of the event and stored for years within the mind-body system – starts to find a healthy way of releasing.

When enough time has been given for this part of the exploration, I invite people to imagine another child, sitting in the left palm, saying, "This is a healthy child whose joy and creativity is not spoiled. She is always ready to play with you. She has not been scarred by our system of education. Look in her eyes, talk to her, listen to her...."

With this simple exercise, people can begin to understand how the creative impulse has been stifled and how it can be reclaimed.

All in the Same Boat

At the start of a new Primal workshop, it's a good strategy to invite people to introduce themselves to each other through gibberish, which is speaking nonsense or using language they don't know and also by using their hands to communicate what cannot be conveyed through linguistics. This helps people become looser, more expressive, less pretentious.

The contrast is clearly visible. When I tell people, "Now switch to using English," the energy in the room immediately changes. Things become stiffer. Fun and friendliness are replaced by old habits of hiding behind protocol or introducing oneself in superficial ways. Already, through this simple exercise, people start becoming aware of how they inhibit their spontaneity and vitality.

15

Next, I explain the importance of group-sharing. Osho says, "If you hide yourself from others, by and by, hiding becomes part of your nature. Then you can't come out from this habit of hiding."

So, to create an understanding about the importance of sharing is one of the main foundations of working with people in a group. If you understand the importance of not hiding, you will soon be able to pinpoint the psychological issue that is affecting you in any given moment. Which means that the problem is almost gone, because exposure is half the journey.

At first, it may seem embarrassing or shameful to relate your personal experiences to others, but soon you start laughing because you realise everyone is in the same boat. So many times, I've heard people say, with relief, "I thought I was the only one with a problem, but actually everybody has the same issue." Then you begin to relax. Then you don't take your personal problems so seriously.

But old habits die hard, as they say, and transforming negative attitudes takes time. In my experience, a group like this requires at least five days to give people a solid understanding of their issues and how to overcome them.

As the days roll by, you experience good moments and bad moments, swinging like a pendulum between the limitations of the past and the freedom of the present, between ingrained habit and spontaneous creativity.

An effective way to gain the depth in sharing circles is to invite people to explore issues arising from their relationships with their parents. I will talk more about this in a later chapter where I'll discuss working with a therapeutic method called Family Constellation.

For now, I will say that the origin of almost all our psychological problems originates in our family relationships. When we have exposed and resolved these original issues we gain peace and fulfilment.

Without Destruction, Nothing New Can Come

Another important element of Primal Painting is to embrace destructiveness; understanding the principle that without destroying the old, nothing new can emerge.

Normally, children are educated to be 'civilised', to preserve and conserve, to be careful not to damage, break or destroy things. We teach them that the impulse to destroy is bad, even though these same children may be fed a daily diet of all types of destructive behaviours on television. So, the messages they receive might be really mixed.

My perspective is that without destruction nothing new can come into existence. So, in this workshop I include a session where each participant is given a sheet of white paper – good quality, costly paper – and then told to behave like a child who has been given total freedom.

Usually, people start out in a careful way, making paper boats, or hats, or delicate origami artworks. Some are enjoying touching the paper with their fingers, or smelling it, or listening to the sound it makes when you shake it.

This is a good beginning because I want people to be aware of this careful, conserving attitude toward creativity; not wanting to go too far, keeping safe – like guarding a bank balance.

After pointing out this tendency and putting on an audio of a giggling child, things start to loosen up. Soon, someone has made a hole in the paper and is poking his head through. Then one guy starts ripping the paper and throwing little balls at people and immediately this has a wildfire effect. Everyone goes crazy, bits of paper are flying everywhere. It's like a snowstorm in the hot season of India.

However, there are a few participants who are unable to enjoy this act of tearing up paper and going wild and this is sometimes because of their strict upbringing of children – they may have not been allowed to be 'irresponsible'. Here, I make sure they understand how deeply the morality was imprinted on their young minds – not to waste things, not to damage costly goods. Otherwise, when we were small, we simply enjoyed destroying merely for the sake of it.

At a certain point, I become very strict and say, "Stop! I didn't tell you before, but I have invited your parents to this workshop. They are standing here beside me. Now what are you going to do?"

Of course, the wild, chaotic energy disappears. People are frozen. They forget about play. They feel guilty. Some even start trying to clean up the mess. An air of seriousness, even gloom, descends on these 'children'. Here, I ask people to remember the actual words their parents used in this kind of situation and they can easily do so: "Don't make such a mess! Don't be so childish! Grow up! How dare you waste such expensive paper! You're in trouble now! You'd better clean this up before your father gets home!"

This session is intended to give people an understanding of how their energy was blocked and how to regain their original vital energy. This seems simple and easy, but it is not. The conditioning has gone deep. We were trained to be good, be careful, make sense, give a rational explanation for everything we did.

If you understand this simple dynamic between destruction and creation, you will have a fresh, innocent mind which can respond to any situation.

"It's okay, your parents have gone!" I announce and the playfulness returns.

One of the benefits of this exercise is that people come to understand how destruction is just the other side of the coin of creativity. In fact, no destruction is actually happening. It's just a label that's been slapped on certain kinds of activity, which society condemns as unproductive, wasteful, or useless. We are bringing awareness to those labels to reclaim the energy behind them.

Garbage or Mystery: What You See is Up to You

In the end, I ask them to gather all the pieces of paper in the middle of our space and form a circle around the pile.

"What do you see?" I ask.

"Garbage," comes the answer.

Most people, looking at such a 'mess' would agree. This is the way we have been trained to see things. But there is another way of looking - looking without prejudice. You can see things with innocent eyes, as if for the first time in your life. If you can shift from the head to the heart, you make new discoveries.

This introduces a way of meeting life with a fresh attitude and this, in turn, serves two purposes: to look at life without carrying learned attitudes and to discover a new kind of beauty in painting.

"Garbage…well, that's our normal way of looking at something like this," I respond. "If you soften your gaze and allow the garbage to look at you, rather than you looking at the garbage, you may be in for a surprise."

19

The scene is the same, but the transformation is profound. To help with the transition, I invite people to hold hands and then walk slowly in a clockwise direction, looking with a soft gaze at the heap of the papers in the middle of our circle. As we move, the shapes keep changing and our visual sensitivity grows.

"I see contrasts of light and dark...I see sculptures...an iceberg floating in the sea...a mountain rising from the plains...the light is beautiful on all this white..."

When we look with innocent eyes, without our usual interpretation, we may be astonished by the wealth of creativity to be found in such a simple thing: a pile of torn paper. This is especially important for painters, because it is through accidents - such as the way a few pieces of paper are lying together - that we can enter into new, unknown territory. In this way, we find inspiration everywhere.

If you drop preconceived ideas, simply seeing things as they are, you are bound to discover beauty wherever you look.

Chapter Three

Exchanging Paintings

It is time to give my participants a challenge, in which they are invited to work on each other's paintings. Normally, in life, we don't do things like this. We feel too possessive to allow such things to happen. After all, we say to ourselves, *"My creativity belongs to me!"* Even though we may know that what we have created on the paper in front of us is not that great, feelings of indignation may arise: how dare you step into my territory!

This is a classic exercise with many aspects, touching all kinds of emotions, and there is much to be learned from it. All kinds of insights can be gained and that's why I use it in Primal Painting. We are motivated to look inside and inquire: where are these feelings coming from? What is the reason we can't share with other people? Why do we cling to what we create? Is it because we fear losing something of ourselves? Is it because we have stumbled upon the same basic mechanism that causes us to hang onto our problems, which, in turn, gives us a sense of identity?

This is a beauty of working as a group. It is difficult to get out of one's way alone because we have so many blind spots, so many layers of personality that we can't see, and these tend to block our way. But working with other people gives us many mirrors, many reflectors through which to understand ourselves.

This is the key: to come out of isolation as a separate entity, to expose our darkness and open up to others, realising that everybody is connected in some way or other and nobody is an island; we are part of one Earth.

My Way of Painting

The main thing I want people to grasp from the exercise is that during childhood, out of eagerness to be accepted, approved or admired, they learned to paint in a certain way. Now, as adults, they believe that *this is it*. This is 'my way' of painting. This is 'my style', and 'my creativity'.

Without knowing what is coming, I invite participants to spontaneously create a painting and then, when they have done so, I guide them to explore their connection with it.

"How do you relate with your painting?" I ask. "Do you like it? Is there a sense of achievement and attachment?"

I explain the common tendency that as soon as a particular shape, colour or certain kind of expression appears on the paper then, from that moment onwards, we avoid interfering with it. We focus on filling in the blank areas and, as soon as the paper is filled with colour and shapes, we simply say, "It's finished!"

We are not aware that we have become a kind of slave to the painting.

But for me, painting is not like that. It is a journey to your depth. When you touch the depths of your being, then whatever you paint will show the same depth. That's why the following exercise is significant: one starts seeing one's own limitations.

When the participants have had time to produce something substantial and significant, I ask them, "Are you ready for an adventure? Are you ready to learn that something else is possible for you?" Then I explain the exercise: they are going to exchange paintings with the person sitting next to them and continue to paint on his or her creation, adding to what has already been done.

"Are you ready to be disturbed by your partner?" I ask the group. "Are you ready to come out of your comfort zone?"

It's important for people to understand that this exercise isn't just an invitation to destroy each other's paintings. When you bring awareness to the act of adding to another person's painting, then it has a different connotation, a different quality. For sure, an element of destruction is inevitable, because the painting will be changed and in a certain sense the original creativity will be lost, the past will be gone. But at the same time, both partners will grow through the shared experience.

It may be shocking to see what has been done when the painting is returned to you. It's bound to be a surprise, because people are so different; they approach painting from many different angles, with many levels of awareness and also with different degrees of attachment. Some artists are beginners, others are talented, and others regard themselves as professionals. Some are cautious and careful, others dive in and splash colours with abandon – it's all a big mix and nobody is given time to select an appropriate partner whom they think will not spoil their painting.

So, it can be a shock. But without shock, nothing is likely to happen. The cage surrounding our creativity will remain unbroken.

Profound Experiences

During this two-hour exercise, people go through many profound experiences. For example, one initial reaction, which is very common, is to sit in front of the other person's painting and say, "Oh no, I can't do anything!"

Why not? It's worth taking a deeper look. Usually, it's because a wound of inferiority is being touched; a psychological complex is being encountered, a comparison is being made in which we consider ourselves to be less talented, or less creative than others. In this moment, faced with the task of changing another's painting, the task seems overwhelming – "Any action on my part is bound to have a disastrous effect on what has already been done."

With this kind of attitude, people just sit and pretend to paint, afraid to interfere. Later, when justifying this approach, they excuse it as 'respect' for the other's creation.

Another response is to experience greater freedom than when working with our own paintings. This easily turns into license and carelessness: "This painting does not belong to me, so I'm free to do what I like." Usually, this kind of attitude will be more destructive than creative because it ignores the invitation to be sensitive and to look deeper.

Whatever the attitude of the one who is adding to the painting, it will be of benefit to the one whose painting is being changed. No one ever comes out of the comfort zone by repeating old habits and patterns. By being disturbed, one becomes aware of what one was avoiding and missing.

The process is rather like gestalt therapy, in which you learn to take back responsibility for conflict with another person. Rather than blaming the other for creating hell for you, you turn the energy around and start asking, "What is going on inside me? Who creates such a fight?"

In This Moment

With awareness, participants can get past these initial tendencies. They can use the opportunity presented by exchanging paintings to expand, to open and to explore the question: "What is my quality in this moment? What is new for me? How does my energy want to express itself, right now?"

Some people discover a genuine wildness in themselves that is not destructive but liberating: "I don't dare do this to my own painting, but I can explore it here." Others may discover new depths of creative sensibility: "I need to take care, so I will take more time to tune in and express what I feel on a deeper level."

When participants return to their own paintings and look at what has been done, the first reaction is almost always: "No! Somebody has destroyed my creation! Somebody didn't respect me! Somebody just dumped colours on my beautiful painting!"

Many people become angry and I support this emotion by introducing the next step in the structure. Standing facing each other, with their paintings on the floor between them, the two partners are invited to take turns in saying, "I don't like what you did to my painting!" One listens while the other speaks; then, after 5-10 minutes, they change roles.

It seems like a simple exercise, but in ordinary life few people give themselves the opportunity to express their negativity in such a clear and direct manner. Rather, people tend to keep on stuffing down their objections until one day they explode in anger. Then communication is not possible. Instead, people feel hurt and misunderstood - this is how we create conflict with each other. So, this is a very different approach.

New Way to Listen

The one who is being addressed does not react to what is being said. It is a neutral space of listening, similar to the technique employed in the process of self-inquiry known as, 'Who is in?'

To simply listen is a valuable experience. Normally, when confronted by an angry person, we resist and fight back. We want to show that we are right and the other is wrong. Or we want to run away, slam the door and say, "I'm not going to listen to this bullshit."

In this exercise, the listening partner stands in a relaxed way, without making facial expressions, keeping eye contact, receiving the other person's negativity without fighting back, while watching the effect this is having inside. When listening in this way, people often report that memories arise from past situations – situations where they did their best, tried hard to do something, then felt rebuffed, rejected or condemned.

Such memories are important. They show us how we contracted, shut down our energy, or turned away from creative effort because it was not welcomed.

Looking back, you may see that a wound occurred at the very moment when your heart was singing and you were in a natural flow of creative energy. Maybe as a small child, you did your best to create a painting for your father, or your mother, but this parent said, "You don't know how to paint," or "You did it the wrong way." Instead of gratitude and appreciation, you received corrections, or advice on how to do it better...well-intentioned guidance that distracted you from yourself.

That's why I offer workshops in Primal Painting, because we are all carrying these patterns and energies from childhood.

Even now, as adults, they find expression in our daily lives, whether at work in the office, or at home with our love partners, or when painting.

Revealing Insights

It is equally as valuable to be the partner who is conveying his or her negativity through exploring the sentence, "I don't like what you did to my painting," as it can lead to surprising insights. For example, focusing on the details of what has been done to your painting, you may find that everything you've been avoiding in your approach to artistic expression – and maybe in your life as a whole – has been revealed in the contribution made by your partner.

Perhaps you were too careful to permit yourself to take risks, whereas now this has been done for you. Perhaps you were too worried about making mistakes, whereas now these 'errors' are clearly visible.

As you can see, this is a simple exercise, but it contains many layers.

When negative energy is expressed and released, a degree of emptiness can be experienced inside. After the storm, a calm spaciousness can be felt. In this empty space, you can begin to accept what the other person did.

Embracing the Positive

This brings us to the next stage of the exercise. One partner says, "I like what you did to my painting!" and explains why this is so, while the other listens.

Surprisingly, almost everybody who said, "I don't like what you did to my painting," can find an authentic way of expressing the positive side.

For example: "I like what you did to my painting because you added black and I was afraid of that. I couldn't do it myself, but now you have done it for me. Because of the darkness, my painting has gained depth."

We see that what we have been rejecting is really an unlived part of our own creative potential. We see that we have been repressing our spontaneity, our willingness to take risks, our curiosity to explore new styles. We have been playing safe, because that's what we learned as children.

Now we are being pushed out of our comfort zone in search for our authentic creative energy. This becomes apparent when we come to the end of the exercise and once more begin to work on our own paintings. This is when we experience a new freedom to go beyond our old ideas about 'my creativity'.

Creativity: Multi-Dimensional Experience

Another important exercise, which is really an extension of the one before, is to sit silently, in a receptive mood, and watch while someone paints on your painting. Here, you are absorbing the surprises, the mysterious twists and turns, that creativity is taking before your eyes. Someone else is painting but you are also participating because you have done the groundwork from which this person is building.

Creativity is a multi-dimensional experience. It is not just action. Action may be a beginning, a first step – throwing colours on paper, disturbing each other, dancing, playing – but receptivity and silent witnessing takes the creative experience much deeper.

There is a profound relationship between receptivity, innocence and meditation. In fact, the child-like space of innocence that I have referred to many times in this book can be more easily accessed through meditation than anything else.

What is innocence? It is freedom from knowledge, freedom from preconceived ideas and attitudes. It is a clean, clear mind that is open to the freshness and the surprise that this moment brings.

I remember Osho saying, "Creativity is the fragrance of individual freedom."

To find your creativity, you must find your freedom, and this is why meditation is an important element in my work. Meditation is the art of emptying the mind, of learning how to be silent and receptive. The mind may continue to chatter by itself, but you are not caught up in it.

You are a witness; you can sit and watch the mind, just as you can sit and watch someone painting on your painting, without getting disturbed.

The Quality of Presence

When you facilitate as an art therapist, you recognise the preciousness of the quality of presence that arises out of a meditative space. Being able to observe your body, your thoughts, your emotions, while connecting with your heart and giving expression to your own intuition…this is the foundation of creating presence.

If you can act out of this space of awareness, then whatever you do is right. And it will reach to the hearts of the people with whom you are working. Presence means you are no more carrying the past, you are fully present, here and now.

You don't look at the other as a problem, but as a potential. You will give back the other's dignity. You will trust the other as you trust yourself.

Always, the starting point is you. Your quality of meditation is all that really counts. If you are relating only through the mind, your clients will also stay in the mind. And if you are radiating your joy, others will catch the flavour of that.

In the work of Osho Therapy, the understanding of 'helping' is different. The client is not a patient, but more like a friend on the same journey. You share yourself like a sunbeam – if the flowers start blossoming in this light, it is not your concern. It is just a side effect of being yourself. Our tendency of wanting to be a 'helper' in the conventional way probably originates with the early psychological state of a child who wants to help his or her parents, but is helpless to do so.

In this regard, it is valuable to re-introduce the systemic work of Family Constellation, which I will talk more about later in the book. I have seen many cases where problems between therapists and clients can be traced back to the relationships within the original family.

Innocence and Ignorance

By the way, I should point out a small but important difference between the innocence of a child, who is just a child, and the child-like innocence of an adult. A child's innocence has the flavour of ignorance. He doesn't know anything. He can be fresh and alive because he has not yet been filled with beliefs, ideas, knowledge. So, in a way, his innocence is waiting to be corrupted, which seems inevitable in our kind of society.

An adult who reclaims the space of innocence is completing the circle. He, or she, has been through the whole process of education, of gaining knowledge, of being stuffed with all kinds of social nonsense, but has found a way back to a child-like space.

In my workshop, it's a two-way process: innocence helps you deepen your artistic capacity as a painter; and painting, as I teach it, helps you to re-experience what innocence is like. That's the beauty of Primal Painting.

Chapter Four

Saying 'Yes' and Saying 'No'

'Yes' and 'No' are two of the most important words in our lives, maybe *the* most important. If we were told that we could have only two words, out of the whole range of language, to guide us through life, we'd probably choose these two.

If we don't have a 'yes' to life, we can only shrink and die. If we do not know how to say 'no', we will have no personal boundaries and no will of our own.

In my understanding of how people develop, it's important to be able to say 'yes' and 'no' in a wholehearted way; to say them and mean them, not just verbally but with our full energy. Half-hearted expressions won't do.

And of course, since art reflects life, this ability to say 'yes' and 'no' is essential when painting. So, it's an important part of my training.

A Limited 'Yes'

It's worth remembering that, in our early stages of life, we had to say 'yes' before we learned to say 'no'. We had no choice. As small babies, we were helpless, totally dependent on our parents. We bonded to our protectors and did whatever they wanted with the minimum of fuss – or, maybe sometimes with a lot of fuss. But, basically, we said 'yes'.

In a small baby, there is nothing wrong with such a 'yes'. It's a necessary stage of development. But when this kind of 'yes' carries on into adolescence and adult life as an ingrained habit, it can become a big limitation, even crippling personal growth.

For example, if we obey authority in a mechanical way – saying 'yes' to teachers, employers and superiors out of fear, or duty, or just to get a pay-check at the end of the week – then our 'yes' has no guts in it. There is no energy behind it. Any 'yes' that comes from this source is going to be half-hearted, mediocre, and will not allow us to experience the full range of our possibilities as a creative human being.

Nor do we need the kind of 'yes' developed through the American psychology of 'positive thinking'. The 'yes' I am talking about is not a strategy. It's not something to learn and practise because it pays off. It's not a tool for fulfilling personal ambition. It's a natural part of being plain, simple, authentic human beings.

A Limited 'No'

Being able to express a wholehearted 'no' is equally important although some people find it strange when they first come to me. This is because they've been taught to suppress the 'no', by smiling and saying 'yes'.

The feeling that we have the power and ability to say 'no' forms a big part of our sense of personal freedom. It's an essential element in the process that some psychologists call 'establishing healthy boundaries' that we need for our everyday interaction with each other.

Learning to say 'no' starts early, between the ages of two and four years old. Theoretically, at least, every child emerges from this stage proud of his independence, feeling self-assured and excited about the degree of control he has over his life.

Of course, it doesn't always work. Even the best parents will need to override the child's 'no' in certain situations: *"Johnny, get up now, it's time for school."*

"No, Mum, I don't want to."

"You have to go to school. Now get up, or I'll fetch your father."

So, reluctantly, Johnny gets up and goes to school. Such experiences serve as a vital part of a child's exploration of 'no' and its limits.

A Deeper 'No'

There is a deeper 'no' in all of us that has its roots in our social history. Past generations were trained much more strictly in obedience than we are today. Everyone 'knew his place' in society and was expected to conform to a fixed hierarchy of power and authority. Economics played a big part, because jobs were handed down through families, through guilds, through tight social groups, and not many people were able to break out and try something new.

This has been changing, particularly over the last hundred years, and especially for women. Economic growth, exploding technology and greater mobility have created so many different job opportunities that we no longer feel so enslaved, so compelled to do what others tell us to do.

Yet we carry the collective memories of those earlier times. They sit inside us, as a layer in our psychology – a deep resentment at being forced to do or say things we did not like. So, even though modern society has given us more personal freedom than at any time in history, we tend to be suspicious of people who encourage us to say 'yes'.

We may even feel as if we are going to be exploited. Therefore, even when we do say 'yes', it's usually done cautiously, with a 'no' hiding just behind it.

Getting 'Behind' an Action

In daily life, we try to ignore the fact that we have an ongoing struggle inside us between 'yes' and 'no'. Yet at the same time, we do recognise the importance of being clear and decisive: Is it a 'yes' that I feel, or is it a 'no'?

To help my participants get a sense of this, I invite them to choose a partner and explore my Art Critic exercise. One partner is a painter, hoping to exhibit his, or her, work. The other is an art critic, looking for talented new artists for an exhibition of modern art at the famous Bilbao Guggenheim Museum in Spain.

In this small psychodrama, the function of the critic is to be intellectual, knowledgeable and rational, with a head full of judgements. The painter must try to convince the critic that his, or her, painting is worth considering for the exhibition.

The point of the exercise is to encourage the painter to get behind his painting, to talk about it with passion and enthusiasm. He must hold it up for the critic to see and explain why it is such a great work of art.

It's surprising how powerful this exercise can be, especially for the painter. After all, it's certainly true that no painting exactly like this one has ever existed on the Earth before and through this understanding one can start seeing the beauty and uniqueness of creation.

The critic may also be touched. When someone is talking so passionately about his creativity, you are bound to become interested. The painter's excitement will connect the critic with more vitality and more life energy.

In painting, as in other activities, if you are really *behind* what you are doing, if you're giving your total energy to it, without hesitation, then whatever you do will work. If you are half-hearted, nothing really works. At the most, you may accomplish a technically adequate painting, but there will be no fire, no soul, no poetry in it.

Saying 'Yes' with Dignity

Unless you can say 'yes' with dignity, there's no real progress in spiritual growth. So, the question needs to be asked: how do we come to this state of 'yes'? Can it be experienced through the medium of painting? As I see it, this is one of the most important elements in a training – to create a situation where participants can see if a 'yes' is coming from an authentic space.

One practical and powerful method is to introduce the exercise of exchanging paintings that I described earlier. Let us look at it again, from a slightly different perspective. First, in order to create the right context, I invite people to paint alone. Normally, when they do this, they feel a certain contentment within themselves, because even though they are aware of their limitations, they enjoy the act of creativity and feel they are connecting, to a certain degree, to a space of 'yes'.

When I invite them to exchange paintings, you can guess what happens in terms of 'yes' and 'no'. Many people want to say, "No! This is my painting!" but they have agreed to explore with me, so they exchange paintings and continue the exercise.

Later, when they stand facing each other, their paintings on the floor, saying, "I don't like what you did to my painting!" What is actually happening? They are strengthening their ability to say 'no'.

Embracing the Positive

In the next stage of the exercise, when they say, "I like what you did to my painting!" the change in gestalt has a remarkable impact. In addition to the 'no', a sense of 'yes' arises that is genuine and heartfelt.

When you say 'yes' within the context of having the freedom to say 'no', a revolution occurs and you can see how your painting has gained from the exchange.

The structure of the exercise now becomes clear: 'no' creates the foundation from which 'yes' opens the doors of creativity and expansion.

'Yes' is such a huge word when it comes from deep within us, because it means 'yes' to life, 'yes' to existence, 'yes' to yourself, 'yes' to beauty, 'yes' to everything. 'Yes' is a key to holistic and healthy expression. 'Yes' is magic.

If I Say 'Yes' to Myself in This Moment

There are many ways to support this kind of alchemical transformation. For example, another method I use in my trainings is the technique of 'saying yes to myself in this moment', which I learned from my friend and colleague Sagarpriya DeLong Miller.

Again, it's a simple method. To begin, I simply suggest to people that they don't do anything special, but continue as they are; perhaps sitting, doing nothing, or drinking a cup of tea, or walking around the room, or scratching an arm...

"Don't do anything different," I tell them. "Just add a sentence, speaking aloud, describing what you are doing. For example, you might say: 'If I say 'yes' to myself in this moment, I am putting my right foot in front of my left foot...'"

By bringing awareness to whatever action is happening – drinking, sitting, walking, brushing your teeth – you are brought directly into contact with the present moment. You are also brought into a greater awareness of your physical body.

The human mind has a great capacity to take us away from the present moment. It tends to live either in past memories or future expectations, hopes and dream, so we rely on habit to perform various daily functions while we mentally disconnect from the body, drifting away on a chain of thoughts about other things.

This exercise not only brings you into the present; it supports you in saying 'yes' to the present and to ordinary daily activity. This knack of becoming present to yourself is of great value when painting, because you develop the habit of tuning into yourself – your energy, your feelings – before putting brush to paper.

However, I need to make it clear that I am not teaching people to say 'yes' as a form of 'positive thinking'. It's not about looking on the bright side of life, which to me is a kind of self-hypnosis. It's not an attitude to life or a particular belief. It's about tuning into yourself at deeper and deeper levels, accepting whatever you find to be true and bringing it into the light of your own awareness.

We're here to be authentic human beings...plain, simple, natural. We're here to sing a song with nature and invite rainbows into our lives through painting.

Reflecting Inner Attitudes

Art therapy is an exploration of both 'yes' and 'no'. The way you pick up a paint brush and use it on a canvas reflects the two impulses inside you and whether or not they are in conflict.

To any experienced therapist, your inner state will be immediately revealed, not in specific detail, not in the anecdotes of your personal history, but in the condition of your energy. This, in turn, will vividly expose your attitude and outlook towards life.

Do you hesitate before dipping the brush in the paint and making a stroke? Do you feel as if it is impossible to capture the beauty of nature on paper, no matter how hard you try? Do old memories surface, along with critical voices from teachers or parents, making you feel, "I can't do this...I'm not a painter...I'll never be able to create anything beautiful..." etc?

These are just a few examples of the kind of reactions people experience when they pick up a paint brush. With time and persistence, we may learn to ignore some of these voices and achieve the goal of producing a painting, but still, underlying attitudes may continue. For example, having learned a certain technique that produces results, we may be afraid to try anything new, lest we destroy what we've accomplished; or, we may stick to 'safe' colours and subjects that do not challenge our deeper insecurities.

Connecting with Power

'Yes' to painting and 'yes' to ourselves go hand-in-hand. They are one and the same thing. So, when we invite people to say 'yes' to painting, we are also extending an invitation to say 'yes' to life.

At first, you may think it strange to address the issue of saying 'yes' to your own life. After all, who doesn't want to live? And yet the *way* we live shows how much we have compromised in order to survive and get along with others. We have reduced our 'yes' from a shout to a whisper.

What does it mean to say 'yes' to painting? It means that, in an atmosphere of trust and safety, people can connect with their energy, their creativity, their strength and power, and give all of these qualities dynamic expression through painting.

It means they can heal the psychological wounds that inhibit free and spontaneous expression. It means that, through the medium of painting, they can become more whole and healthy human beings.

There is an ancient expression: 'Art imitates life'. Nobody seems to know where it comes from, but Oscar Wilde turned the saying on its head with his famous comment that "Life imitates art far more than art imitates life."

From a therapeutic standpoint, both of these sayings are relevant, but neither of them are accurate. The truth is, art *reflects* life, and the way an artist goes about his work reflects the very life of that artist.

It avoids using the intellect and, with it, all the opportunities for self-deception that the clever, rationalising human mind offers. The paint brush never lies. It is a faithful mirror, accurately reflecting one's inner reality.

Following Without a True 'Yes'

As an art therapist, it's my job to help people grasp the importance of saying 'yes', but it can't be done simply through words and explanations.

For example, about half-way through a recent five-day international course on nature painting, I noticed that a 40-year-old Japanese woman called Kiyomi was good at following instructions. She was willing to accept guidance, but her painting had a mechanical quality to it.

She was saying 'yes', but her energy wasn't connected with what she was doing.

I could see that trying to change Kiyomi's approach would be a delicate matter. She was a shy, quiet person, lacking in self-confidence, so any personal comments would be perceived as criticism. This would further damage her self-confidence and inhibit any development in her painting style.

What to do? I opted for a general approach. I called the group together and introduced a beautiful metaphor, originally created by Friedrich Nietzsche, using the symbols of a camel, a lion and a child. It's a metaphor that Osho talked about many times in his discourses as a way to illustrate our human condition and potential.

The camel symbolises obedience. He automatically does what he is told, like a dutiful beast of burden, saying 'yes' to whatever is asked of him. He is a faithful servant of authority.

The lion symbolises rebellion. He reacts to external authority with a loud 'no' that proclaims his individuality. He impulsively rejects being told what to do.

The child symbolises freedom. His response is not predetermined by an automatic 'yes', nor a compulsive 'no'. When the child says 'yes' it is out of his inner sense of freedom, so his energy will be behind his word. If he says 'no' it is because this represents a true expression of his energy in the moment – not a reaction against being told what to do.

After explaining the metaphor, I told the group, "As a teacher, I have certain things to say to you, skills to pass on to you, because, after all, this is a painting training. As a student, there are three ways to learn: you can follow my suggestions automatically, you can react against what I'm telling you, or you can be the child.

"Each moment, the child asks himself: 'Where am I right now, in my personal process? Does it feel right for me to experiment with what the teacher is saying? If she suggests that I use stronger colours, do I have a 'yes' for it, or would I rather try something else?'"

Then I invited the participants to form into pairs and assign themselves the roles of teacher and student. The person playing 'teacher' was then invited to make a series of critical comments, or suggestions, while the 'student' was painting. For example:

"Your colour tones are flat; why don't you add a complementary colour?"

"Your hand movement is mechanical. Why aren't you more innovative?"

"You're not watching nature while you are painting it..."

The student was invited to explore all three ways of responding: as a camel, a lion and a child. The atmosphere in the room soon became playful as the participants enjoyed acting out the roles, especially the lion, which gave them freedom to say 'no' in ways that are not normally allowed in a classroom.

When the 'student' had experienced all three, the partners switched roles and repeated the experiment. Afterwards, in a group-sharing session, many participants reported that they were able to recognise their tendencies and habits.

Kiyomi said nothing, but in the days that followed, I noticed a significant change in her approach to painting, which became more dynamic and alive. She had understood the point and was now *behind* her 'yes'.

Chapter Five

Partner Painting

How do we discover and express what is hidden inside us? How do we let go of our limited identity? We've talked about exchanging paintings and becoming more aware through a negative reaction – "I don't like what you did to my painting."

We saw how such reactions point to qualities that may be missing in our own personal expression. Now we can go a little further through the structure of partner painting.

I guide people to choose a partner. There are two ways to choose. One is to find someone whose energy matches your own. This is the easiest and safest route, because if the other person is like you then nothing much can go wrong; the risk of conflict and misunderstanding is minimised.

This person will accept you as you are; this person will dance in the same way, paint in the same way, and this person will be hiding the same things that you are hiding. Naturally, you will feel safe, cosy and comfortable.

The other way is to choose the kind of person you usually avoid. In a workshop situation you can easily find such people, because you instinctively turn away from them, keeping a distance, making sure they don't come too close.

With this kind of person, you're more likely to see what you've been avoiding in your creative expression – how and in what way you're saying 'no'.

Sometimes, people enjoy a challenge like this. Sometimes they are not ready.

I encourage my participants to respect their boundaries, noticing how open they are to others. So, they have the option: they can start the easy way, choosing someone safe, then later, when they're feeling stronger and more grounded, take on a bigger challenge. Or, they can jump right away and choose a difficult partner.

What Are Your Judgements?

For the purpose of this chapter, let's say they've chosen a challenging partner, someone whom they would normally avoid.

First, I guide the two partners to stand facing each other, looking into each other's eyes.

Then I ask, "What are your judgements about this person?"

To our normal, polite, social way of thinking, this may sound like a strange question. The rational mind may object: "I hardly know this person, so why should I judge?" However, the truth is that our judgements arise very quickly. We need only look at a person to immediately form an opinion:

Attractive...unattractive...too   loud...too   quiet...too fat...too thin...too ugly...too proud...too nice...too nasty...

It happens in an instant. And certainly, when we choose someone whom we dislike, or someone of whom we are afraid, such opinions are bound to be present. After all, these are the reasons why we have avoided contact.

One thing I make clear before the exercise: all judgements belong to you. Your partner is just a screen, a reflection, because you are looking at a stranger. You may have formed an impression, based on brief acquaintance; or perhaps he, or she, reminds you of your mother or father...but you don't really know this person sitting in front of you.

The next thing to understand is that the judgements that you are directing at this person are an indication of something you are rejecting or denying in yourself. Again, it may sound a little strange, because in normal society we are in the habit of continuously expressing opinions about other people. All gossip is like that. All our favourite newspapers, magazines and TV programmes are full of it. We never pause to think that, on some deep level, we're talking about ourselves.

"This is a valuable opportunity, not an easy moment, to be sure, but full of potential," I tell participants. "If you're ready to take responsibility for your judgements, to *own* them, to take them back and look inside yourself, then you have a good chance to see what it is you've been hiding."

Bridging the Communication Gap

When people react to each other, get into a fight or an argument, what are they doing? They are throwing their judgements onto the other person. I criticise you, you criticise me, I blame you, you blame me...it's a game of ping-pong that never ends and, as a result, the two people involved may never really meet.

But when you accept your negative opinions as your own, then your whole mental attitude changes. As a result, the quality of communication with the other person is also bound to change. A bridge may open between two islands that were separate and alienated.

Once people have understood how the process of judgement works, I invite them to leave their partner and walk around the room, meeting other participants, stopping for a moment, making eye contact and noticing what thoughts come into their minds.

"As you face each person, notice what you're thinking," I instruct. "Become aware of the opinions you are projecting on this person. There's no need to talk. Recognise the thoughts that come into your mind, understand that they belong to you, bow down to this person, walk on, meet another...and so on."

After meeting half-a-dozen people in this way, I invite everyone to find their original partner again and stand facing each other once more.

"You are probably thinking that a meeting with this person will not be possible," I comment. "And who knows? You may be right! But let's explore the situation."

After inviting them to choose who is Partner A and who Partner B, I ask Partner A to stand passively and silently, with eyes closed, doing nothing. Partner B then stands behind Partner A.

Exercise: Seaweed Dance

Already, this simple shift changes the dynamic in the relationship. Now it's no longer a face-to-face confrontation. Partner A is, in a way, helpless, so Partner B has the opportunity to become more sensitive. This leads into the 'seaweed' structure that will emphasise both roles.

"Partner A is seaweed, growing from a rock under the sea," I explain. "Partner B is the water that ebbs and flows around the rock, moving the seaweed this way and that."

I encourage Partner A to become receptive and passive, while inviting Partner B to adopt the role of the active, motivating force. For example, a light push by Partner B on the left shoulder sends Partner A's body swaying to the right; a gentle push from the front sends the body leaning backwards...and so on.

"Seaweed has no resistance and no will of its own," I tell partner A. "It follows the currents, the flow of the water, so just let your body move in response to your partner's touch. This will help you become more aware of a quality of receptivity in you."

After a few minutes, the partners change roles and now it is Partner B's turn to be the seaweed and become receptive, experiencing what it feels like inside to let go of control.

Partner Painting

At this point, when the pairs have played both roles in the seaweed exercise, the group is ready to move into partner painting. Partner A sits in front of a large piece of art paper, which is lying on the floor, and closes his or her eyes. Paints, inks, brushes and water are available near the paper.

Partner B sits close to Partner A, usually to the side because this makes it easy to guide the hands of Partner A, although some people prefer to sit directly behind.

Then Partner B takes one of Partner A's hands – it can be either one – and guides this passive hand to pick out a brush. Next, Partner B guides the hand so that the brush dips into the colours and then begins to paint on the paper.

When a few brush strokes have been made and the colours are on the paper, Partner B tells Partner A to open his eyes and look. It is like a snapshot, a quick photographic glimpse, which has the effect of making a vivid impression. After a few seconds, Partner B tells Partner A to close his eyes again.

He then takes the hand holding the brush back to the paints, dipping into new colours before returning once again to the paper.

"All you're going to say is, 'Open your eyes' and 'close your eyes'. These are the only sentences you say to this person," I explain to Partner B. "You're going to guide this person into a wonderland in which colours are magically appearing in front of his eyes."

I encourage Partner A to pay close attention to what happens, inside as well as outside, because this is a unique opportunity. Partner A is going through the motions of painting, doing all those familiar things he might usually do when he paints, but has no control over the way it is happening.

Freedom and Resistance

"When your partner is guiding you, what is happening to you?" I inquire. "Do you resist? Can you relax and let go? Are you discovering something new, which you haven't known until now? How much freedom, how much space, can you give to this new experience and how much are you preoccupied with resistance?"

I give plenty of time for the partners to explore painting in this way, then ask them to change roles and begin again. They experience both roles: active and passive.

After the exercise, when I invite feedback, many participants talk about their resistance to being guided. After all, it's natural. We are accustomed to being completely in control when we paint and this way of painting with a partner is something totally unfamiliar:

"I allowed it to happen...I allowed myself to be guided...but still I felt some resistance because usually I don't choose this particular colour...usually I don't move my hand in this way...usually I don't mix certain colours together..." This is how the feedback goes.

However, many people also taste the joy of surrendering to the guide, enjoying the sense of surprise it can bring:

"I was surprised at how much I was able to cooperate...I was so available to my partner's guidance! I discovered a totally different quality of colours...this way of mixing the paint with water can be beautiful..."

Taken into the Unknown

You may not have thought about it, but it's a precious experience to be taken into the unknown. It's not something we easily do by ourselves, simply because we tend to be creatures of habit, staying with what is familiar. We learn a certain way of painting, somehow it works well enough to produce results...and we stick with it.

But if you have the courage to choose a partner who is different from you, if you can allow yourself to surrender to this person, then you are automatically carried into an unknown space, painting in a way you have never done before.

The active partner also moves into an unfamiliar space. There is a person sitting next to you who is willing to do exactly what you want. It carries a certain responsibility and it makes people more alert, more present and more sensitive.

What is important in both roles is for people to come into the space of the present moment, because when we are really present, really here and now, with our full attention and energy, then we discover that the present carries with it the power of joy, surprise, expansion. Something outrageous can happen, because we are rediscovering the quality of innocence; we go into the space of a young child, remembering what it is like to play and explore without fear.

49

Dancing in Communion

To me, this exercise is amazing. I never tire of guiding people through this experience. In a short time, it gives people an understanding of what they've been avoiding and – as I've already indicated – this is essential in the development of any individual's artistic expression.

Another quality that emerges is a sense of dancing with your body, because when one is guiding and the other is allowing himself to be guided, it is a kind of dance – a duet. As the active partner, your whole body is involved: you have to take the hand of your partner, reaching for the paints, moving the brush over the paper...soon you start to feel a kind of synchronicity arising between you.

It's a non-verbal form of communication and this really helps, because so much of our chit-chat isn't about communicating at all – in fact, just the opposite. We use it as a way of keeping people at a distance.

In just a few minutes, a small miracle has happened. You began this exercise by nervously choosing someone whom you did not like and then, by the end, you find that you have danced and painted your way into a communion of two spirits.

Chapter Six

Spontaneous Painting

Intuition is an elusive gift. Most people are unaware of its existence. It's not something that is taught in schools or given much attention in our education and upbringing. Yet it often plays an important role in artistic expression and scientific discovery.

It's a spark of intelligence, a flash of insight, an impulse to go for the unexpected, a feeling to follow a hunch. It comes out of nowhere, without reason and logic; yet often supplies the missing ingredient that turns creativity into magic.

It was intuition that impelled Vincent van Gogh to abandon conventional ideas about art and paint like no painter had ever done before. It was intuition that made Albert Einstein certain that the laws of natural physics were out of date and a new theory of relativity was required.

Einstein pointed his finger at a major flaw in our education when he said, "The intuitive mind is a sacred gift and the rational mind is a faithful servant. We have created a society that honours the servant and has forgotten the gift."

A Quality in All of Us

I want to tell you that intuition is a human quality that can be embraced by all of us. To find it, to experience it, to remember it, all we need to do is invite this quality into our lives.

One way to help people discover their intuitive nature, I find, is to set up a structure in which the group works with small paintings. It's a simple process: participants are provided with a stack of small pieces of art paper, cut no bigger than the size of a postcard, together with acrylic paints, inks and water. Then, they are invited to paint freely and spontaneously on as many pieces of paper as they wish.

Working with lots of these small pieces of paper immediately reduces the level of expectation. A small painting that is done quickly and casually, which can be thrown away afterwards, reduces the level of personal investment involved. It's not a major project. Obviously, with this kind of set-up, you're not being asked to paint the roof of the Sistine Chapel, or even to make a birthday card for your mother, so already a relaxation happens among the participants.

Big and Small: An Inner Sense

To begin, I give a short demonstration that usually provokes people's objections, which is exactly what I want, since it creates an opportunity to deal with them before the exercise gets under way. For example, a common reaction, when faced with small-sized paper, is to feel contracted, as if one's energy is shrinking. Some people comment, "My freedom will be hindered by the smallness of the paper. I won't be able to dance with my brush. I won't be able to expand."

In response, I relate my experiences with Osho, when I was painting illustrations for books created out of his discourses on Zen.

"At that time, some of my paintings were the size of a matchbox, and on them I still had to put mountains, rivers, bamboos, trees, rocks, rain...," I explained.

This request for miniature paintings didn't come from Osho himself. It came from his team of book designers, who wanted each illustration to be the same size as it would appear in the book, so they could see how it would look when printed.

So, I trained myself in that way and soon came to a new understanding: the sense of big or small has nothing to do with actual size. It's your inner quality, your inner feeling, your inner sense of expansion that determines the stature of any painting.

An Easy Flow

But, as it happens, there aren't many objections from my participants. Mostly, they are relieved and happy to be given a playful project, in which they can paint in a carefree way on these postcard-sized papers.

My intention is to help them experience an easy flow in which they can allow spontaneous freedom of expression, without calculation or hesitation. The guidance I give is simple and straightforward: look at a piece of paper, wait for an inner impulse, express the energy of this moment with a few brush strokes, then put it aside and begin anew. This is how we connect with our intuition, by waiting and listening for the inner impulse that moves us to express something. What comes out may be only one or two broad strokes of colour, but that's perfectly okay – no value judgement is needed.

I remember, during the time I was sending paintings to Osho, he went through a phase of choosing those that were only a wash background, with no object, no form. Even though I'd included them for Osho to see, along with many other styles, I really hadn't expected him to choose them. I considered them to be trivial, lacking depth and significance.

That was an important insight for me, because in my twenties I'd been a great student of art. I studied oil painting, I studied the history of European painting, I visited all the big galleries in all the major cities. And, of course, I'd studied the great Japanese artists before leaving my home country.

In this way, I'd built up a sense of weight, substance and structure around my painting, almost like a cultural context – as if everything I'd ever learned was somehow present in each painting I created.

Perfection of the Present

All of that dissolved when Osho chose those simple 'wash' paintings. It gave me a new understanding: when you're relaxed, when you're spontaneous, whatever is created is always beautiful, always perfect. Why? Because the present moment has its own sense of perfection. Moreover, the present moment is all there is. Existence knows no past, no future. So whatever perfection is to be found in this life, can be found only here and now.

If you're in tune with this present moment, opening to it, cooperating with it, your intuition will show you how to express yourself, and this perfection will manifest in your painting. So, this is what I want people to practise.

Throwing Colours

One more short demonstration is helpful, because I know that, even when the pressure is off and participants are relaxed, some of them – out of habit – will still have a tendency to divide the colours in an organised and systematic way.

That's how we learned art in school: first draw black lines, outlining whatever shapes you want, then paint inside all the delineated areas until the work is 'finished'.

My little pile of paper is stacked beside a large wooden board that is covered with a plastic sheet. I surprise everyone by throwing paint on the board, not on one of the papers. Then I invite everyone to do the same on their own boards.

"This isn't exactly painting," I explain. "We're just throwing colours."

Again, I'm helping people to relax, to get them thinking, "Okay, if it's not really painting then I don't have to worry about form, structure, goals..."

Then I instruct them to take a piece of paper and lay it gently on the colours that have been thrown on the board.

"Now, pick it up and look at the underside. Surprise, there is your painting!"

The participants were not expecting this and are usually delighted by the outcome. A wash of colour has been created in a way that they would never have imagined, or been able to create if they'd been asked to do it in the conventional way.

A Sense of Freshness

For me, it's very important to give people this sense of freshness, innocence and surprise in which they are not 'doers', not wanting to achieve anything, but really just guests witnessing an artistic accident.

"Take another paper and do it again, in the same place, without adding more paint," I continue.

Of course, the second print is going to be similar...and yet significantly different.

The top layer of paint has been taken by the first paper, so now the colours will be more subtle and some parts will remain white because the paint has already gone. This is one way to learn to be sensitive to colours: noticing small differences in shades, hues and patterns between two similar paintings.

At this point, I invite everyone to carefully observe the two little paintings before them because the way the colours melt and merge almost always gives an abstract impression of nature. In some places, the painting may look like a waterfall, in others like a lake, a mountain, a wind, or a sea. In this way, we learn to receive nature into our hearts.

Spontaneity Changes Your Life

Enough guidance. From this moment onwards, I encourage people to explore the process themselves. They can choose to make more paintings in the way just described or to paint directly on the paper. In both cases, I'm inviting them to be spontaneous.

Spontaneity is really one of the most important elements to acknowledge, not only as an artist, but also as a human being, because if you learn the knack of being open to spontaneous feeling, as it manifests in your life, moment to moment, everything will start to change: your relationship with nature, with your relatives, your love partners...it all becomes infused with a new, fresh quality.

Partner Painting with Miniatures

Once the participants are familiar with the process, I introduce new challenges. For example, I ask them to pair up and then swap paintings with their partner each time I ring a bell.

It works like this: you take a blank paper, listen to your impulse and begin to paint. The bell rings, you give the painting away and receive your partner's painting instead. You look, see what your partner has started and respond with your own addition.

If you consider the painting is finished, you put it aside and start a new one, but you continue swapping as you go along. The bell rings every twenty seconds and the process has a beautiful quality because it moves rapidly, so there's really no time to think. People learn to trust their immediate impulses.

This experiment can be expanded. Sometimes, I invite people to gather in circles of six, with each person having their own paints and papers. I ring the bell and they start painting. After 20 seconds I ring it again and they pass their paper to the left. This happens six times until your own painting has travelled all the way round the circle and comes back to you.

But what a transformation! Six people have worked on it, added their style to it. Perhaps you can still recognise it, perhaps you cannot, but certainly you will see all kinds of creative directions that are outside your personal comfort zone.

Transcending Your Limitations

Mind has its limitations. It is also a creature of habit. So, whenever your mind wants to create, it will tend to rely on memories of what you have done before. But in this experiment, there is no opportunity to repeat the old – the new is being done for you! Your partners are helping you to see new possibilities of creativity.

If you really want to be a creator you need to stay open to the pulse of life, which is always new, always changing, always seeking new forms of expression.

In some ways, spontaneity is very similar to the space of being a child, which is one reason why Osho loved Nietzsche's metaphor of the camel, the lion and the child. He saw it as a key to personal transformation.

As camels, we ignore our own intuitive impulse, because we are relying on others to guide us. As lions, we are also unable to go with our intuition, because we are too busy saying 'no' to the commands of others.

As the child, we are not confined to any fixed pattern or habit. We are not driven to say 'yes' or 'no'. We respond spontaneously, intuitively, in the moment. This is true freedom.

Chapter Seven

No Compromise

Saying 'yes' to yourself is the healthiest way to live. It seems to me that if everybody could learn the art of saying 'yes' to themselves, many illnesses from which we are suffering – psychological, emotional and physical – would just go away.

The sad fact is that most of us never say 'yes' to ourselves and this is bound to create stress; it's bound to create difficulties in our lives.

It is well known that in all cultures and in all societies, stretching back for thousands of years, ever since language was invented, we have enjoyed stories and legends about heroes and their courageous deeds. From the myth of Hercules and his impossible tasks, to Sir Lancelot and his quest for the Holy Grail, right up to our present-day movies and the latest James Bond adventure, we have loved and admired heroes.

We love them because they represent an ideal: they have the courage to stand up for themselves and do what they want. They don't compromise. They don't settle for less. They face the challenge, endure the hardships, and succeed in being true to themselves.

Why then do we find it so difficult to emulate them in our own lives? Of course, the answer is clear: because a myth is just a myth, a movie is just a movie. In real life, there's so much more for us to lose and the outcome is never certain.

Conform: The Law of the Jungle

We have a strong need to belong to a group and this is accompanied by a parallel fear of being isolated as an outsider. In some way or other, we are trained from childhood to 'fit in' with everyone else and obey Rudyard Kipling's famous 'Law of the Jungle': *The strength of the Pack is the Wolf, and the strength of the Wolf is the Pack.*

In other words, stick together with your own kind and you'll be safe. For the wolf it may be true, but for us humans it's a little different. We need each other, it's true, but we also feel the urge to assert ourselves as individuals, even if others disapprove or disagree with what we're doing. At such times, we experience the pressure of group conformity as a weight around our necks, holding us back.

My own life provides a good illustration. I was born in Japan, but I've lived outside the country for forty-two years. During this time, I've become a different person and no longer regard myself as 'Japanese'.

But, each time I go back, I can feel myself wanting to be accepted. So, I try to behave like my relatives. I catch myself adjusting to their habits, absorbing their thoughts, going along with their attitudes and opinions.

Dying to the 'Real Me'

This is compromising. It's not a particularly serious situation, because I know that, within a few days, I'll be on a plane and gone. But still, I notice the tendency. And I'm not saying that I ought to be rude, ungrateful for their hospitality, or make it forcefully clear that I'm different. A refusal to comprise doesn't always mean conflict. But I do see that, if I were to continue to remain in 'Japanese mode', so to speak, I would be slowly killing myself, dying to the real me inside.

When we compromise with other people, what happens? Well, for one thing, we are not giving expression to our authentic energy. Rather, we hold back this energy, manipulate it, divert it, contain it...making all kinds of adjustments to fit within the boundaries of a social situation.

But energy that cannot be expressed becomes stagnant, and stagnation is the root cause of sickness. If we are to remain healthy, our energy needs to move and be released in a way that reflects its true nature.

This reminds me of Soseki Natsume, one of the most important and best-loved Japanese writers of the last century. In the beginning of his career, naturally, he was unknown, but his fame grew steadily to the point where he was offered a most prestigious award for his literary achievements.

He refused saying, "I have lived as Soseki Natsume until now, so I will continue to live as Soseki Natsume. Nothing needs to be added to me." He refused an award that every writer in Japan dreams about. What a great way to live life; just being oneself, not allowing anybody to influence you, neither with praise nor condemnation.

Van Gogh: No Compromise

In the world of art, there are many painters who have gone hungry, or suffered hardship, for the sake of their creativity – the starving artist is a historical stereotype of which Vincent van Gogh is one of the most obvious and most famous.

His story is well known. He was supported by his brother Theo, but didn't receive enough money to cover everything – rent, food and art materials – so he starved himself in order to buy the paints he needed.

Van Gogh struck up a friendship with fellow artist Paul Gauguin and in 1888 the two men lived together for a while in the town of Arles, in the South of France, as a way to share ideas and inspire each other.

Gauguin saw himself as a rebellious bohemian, challenging society's values and yet, somehow, he was still seeking public recognition. Van Gogh, on the other hand, saw himself as a monk, completely detached from the social world, pioneering a totally new form of art.

Van Gogh lived in such poverty that Gauguin tried to persuade him to paint in a more acceptable way, to please people, so his paintings would sell. Van Gogh refused and then, of course, the two men fell out. They were trying to live together, to start an artist's commune, but it was impossible. There was no ground on which to meet.

Van Gogh did not have a peaceful life. Seen from the outside, he suffered a lot. He was poor, hungry and lonely, and his art was not accepted or appreciated. But inside himself he was rich and fulfilled in that he was able to give expression to his creative energy.

Osho: Discourses for the Bamboos

I should also put Osho in this category of uncompromising individuals. Every day, in his Pune ashram (now called Osho International Meditation Resort), he would give a morning discourse lasting 90-120 minutes. He was sharing a vision of spirituality, meditation and life that was radical, controversial and at times even shocking.

It wasn't easy for people to be associated with him because he was saying things that went against all traditional religious teachings.

For years and years, he spoke every day, and the number of people who came to listen steadily grew. In the beginning, it was hardly more than fifty; later, it was over a thousand.

One might easily think he was speaking for others and that the size of his audience was important to him. But no. It wasn't like that. He was speaking because this was his individual gift of creativity, the natural expression of his energy. His discourses were his songs.

"Even if nobody is here, I will go on speaking," he said once. "I will talk to the bamboos."

Painting for Myself

I will never forget Osho's comment, because this is the way I would like to paint. Sometimes people ask me to paint this, to paint that, and I need to remember that I'm not painting for anyone except myself. Of course, someone can receive a painting from me - I've given away hundreds of paintings to friends and clients. But when I'm in the act of painting it has to be for myself, in tune with my creative impulse, a natural expression of my own energy.

It wasn't always this way. Up to a certain moment in my life, I was painting for others, especially for my younger sister, Taeko, whom I loved very much; and for Osho, my spiritual Master. Then my sister died and, a few years later, Osho left his body.

I felt disoriented because now there was nobody to address and therefore I had no sense of purpose. I could not dedicate my paintings to anyone. It could have been the end. In fact, it was a new beginning. That was the moment I really clicked with my own energy source. I started painting from my guts - not from my heart out of love for others - but from a much deeper space inside.

Being with Myself

I started using lots of dark colours, which I'd avoided until this point in my evolution as a painter. I was willing to put everything upside down: cherry blossoms growing under water, flowers covered with shadows, a chaos of branches that seemingly had no beginning nor end...introducing elements that according to my rational mind did not fit together. I didn't care anymore.

Still, whenever I finished a painting, I was surprised that I could still see the harmony and the beauty in it. Really, it was a new depth of understanding, because this harmony wasn't created out of knowledge. It was created through being with myself. I was able to stand back, look at a painting and say proudly, "Wow! This is working!"

Exchanging: Playing Safe

I've already spoken about the exercise in which participants exchange paintings in order to connect with an authentic 'no' and an authentic 'yes' inside themselves. I'd like to mention it again because it's also an effective way to experience the desire to compromise.

When you receive your partner's painting and are invited to work on it, all kinds of feelings may be touched. You may become aware that you want to be accepted by this person, liked by this person. You don't want to create turmoil, conflict. You don't want this person to be angry with you. So, you compromise. Rather than tuning into your creative impulse and acting on it, which might result in drastic changes to this painting, taking it in an entirely new direction, you only decorate it. You play safe, adding little bits here and there, going along with the basic structure and the existing colours. You're not at one with your own energy.

Speaking Up for Yourself

The feedback session that is part of this exercise offers another opportunity to see compromise in action. Instead of being honest and saying what you don't like, you may try and package your comments in a nice, acceptable way.

That's when people flake out, turn to me and say, "Honestly, Meera, I can't find anything that I dislike in what my partner has done to my painting. I don't have any negative feelings."

This is a good opportunity to take a deeper look and ask, "Is this really true?"

More often than not, some negative feeling is being suppressed.

I also point out, to these 'nice' people, that the partner may be disappointed, rather than pleased, with this superficial attempt at harmony. They may feel cheated.

I've heard many partners say, "I don't like what you said to me, because you didn't share your energy. You're just going along, following my way. It's not your way."

The Bigger Picture

In this way, my participants start seeing the bigger picture, the looming shape of the social structure surrounding us that demands obedience and conformity.

They begin to see how we are trained to be a shadow of other people; to believe that serving others is the most beautiful way to live; to be humble, to give way to others...and of course to be admired and rewarded for manifesting such selfless qualities in our daily lives.

No teacher points out to his children that, by embracing such values, we are being taught to say 'no' to ourselves.

So, that's why I spend time making sure my participants understand the subtle ways of compromise. It's the enemy of a true artist because, if you compromise, you never connect with your authentic energy. Then whatever you do will be wishy-washy. You won't be satisfied by the results of your creative efforts and your painting will never reach to the hearts of those who look at it.

If you don't like what you do, how can you expect others to like it?

Chapter Eight

Connecting with Your Body and Heart

I am in love with Africa and its people. The country is huge and much of its nature is still wild and untamed. Its people dance in a way that nobody else in the world can match. This is why I encourage my participants, at a certain moment in the training, to become Africans, because it will greatly enrich their paintings.

For me, to be African is to say 'yes' to the qualities intrinsic to the Dark Continent: simplicity, depth and a feeling of having roots that go deep into the earth. This last attribute is particularly important. Without roots, any attempt to create a painting is going to be flat, boring and superficial.

We Belong to the Earth

When I use the word 'roots', of course, I don't mean physical roots. I mean a natural sense of connection between you and the ground on which you walk. If you're not sure what I mean, try taking off your shoes and socks, then walking with bare feet along the seashore, feeling your toes sink into the wet sand. You'll soon get a sense of what I'm talking about.

We humans belong to the earth. We are sustained and nourished by it. We are its children and yet – very much like rebellious teenagers – we have all but forgotten who is taking care of us. We're too busy talking into our mobile phones, playing video games and chatting on Facebook. We don't see ourselves as part of nature any more. So, part of my job is to help people reconnect with their natural roots.

For many years, I've been a student of dance, including everything from classical Japanese to modern European improvisation. When I look at the way Africans move their bodies, I see significant differences from the way other people move. It's not necessarily that they're very active or expressive, although they can be that way; that's how many people think of African dance as something wild, exotic and warlike.

Containing Your Strength

For me, it's a more subtle quality that appeals. As I see it, the movement is contained inside the body in a very special way - as if the rhythm is alive inside and moving of its own accord. These dancers have roots and they have strength, but they're not showing off. Rather, they contain their strength as an earthy quality within themselves.

I was given the opportunity of experiencing this inner dance in a most unusual way. During a trip to the beaches of Goa, I was bodysurfing close to the shore, when a dumper wave picked me up, flipped me upside down, and rammed my head into the sandy bottom.

My neck took the full impact. For days, my neck was so stiff and painful that I couldn't do anything; no writing, no painting, no combing my hair, no turning of my head to look behind me. All I could do was go inside myself and that's how I found the quality of dance that needs no outward movement. It was always there - the inner rhythm, the beat, the music - that was waiting to be discovered.

One performance I will never forget: an African man, just by himself, with no music, continued to dance before a German audience for two hours. He had no special costume, just simple clothes.

His breathing was the music and he managed to keep us entertained, captivated, with his movements the whole time. You need a lot of vitality and a great deal of discipline to be able to do that.

At the end of his performance, he came with a big bowl of water, placed it in the middle of the stage, then danced around it like a woman, swaying his hips...a very feminine dance. I was sitting in the front row and suddenly realised how he was going to end the show, so I covered my head with my coat at the last moment. And sure enough, he threw the whole bowl of water over the audience!

Apart from soaking my coat, he gave me a great gift: a demonstration of totality and beauty through individual expression in dance.

Another African who impressed me came from Senegal. He wasn't a dancer, but the way he walked fascinated me. He was very tall, wore a kaftan robe and his style of walking was almost a dance in itself. As he moved along the street, his body was gently swaying like a tree in the wind - so natural, relaxed and graceful. He wasn't a wealthy man, but he had so much dignity that he seemed like one.

Not Something to be Taught

Early in the training, I encourage participants to experience and enjoy African dancing whenever possible. I help them a bit, because, even though I'm no expert, I can give a few hints and provide opportunities. My trainings are full of dance breaks.

If you watch people at a disco, or at a party, you can see a lot of fancy moves. People have learned these moves, or styles, in order to look good, and you tend to see a great deal of movement with the hands and arms.

69

I call this 'noodle dancing' because if you take a still-photo of each move, then put all the photos together, what you'll see is a bowl of noodles. It's a mess.

When you bring in the African quality, you become more aware of your feet and your pelvis. The feet are the base. Again, I need to mention the powerful connection with the earth because out of this arises the typical African pelvic movement.

It's not something to be taught; it's something your pelvis starts to remember as soon as you stop waving your arms and doing fancy routines. If you know about chakras, then you can say the pelvis is connected to the first chakra, or sex centre. This gives it a raw, primitive, alive and juicy flavour.

Three Secrets

From the pelvis, the movement goes up to the chest, which is another focus of African dance. If you watch, you see the chest comes out in a kind of natural pride; a clear announcement of "Here I am!"

These three places – feet, pelvis and chest – contain all the secrets of African dance. But, as I say, it's not something to be talked about. It's something to be explored.

In this way, my participants learn the power and simplicity of connecting their bodies to the ground beneath their feet because, as I said earlier, this is bound to enrich their paintings. It's also sure to help them in other areas of their lives because vitality is a precious commodity. It colours everything from creativity to relationships to recreation and fun.

It also teaches them the wisdom and power of containment. When it comes to energy, I am all for expression. How can an artist be anything else?

But this needs to be balanced with the ability to stay connected with one's energy inside, as well as throwing it out. Containment does not mean suppression. It is an understanding that, in terms of our relationships with other people, screaming and shouting only cause reaction and misunderstanding. When two people are both reacting, this makes communication very difficult.

Communication happens when you own your energy, taking responsibility for what you feel, and yet contain it. From this space, you can transmit what you want to say without blame. This may allow you to be heard by the other person for the first time.

How to be Italian

Another important step is to teach people how to be 'Italian'. This, for me, introduces a spontaneous quality of the heart. Italians have the capacity to put the head aside and go straight into their feelings. This ability is sure to add a colourful quality to any artist's work.

Of course, I'm not Italian myself, but every year I facilitate a big painting training for children and their parents at the Osho Miasto community in Tuscany. While I'm there, I pay close attention to the way Italians do things. Basically, they don't calculate. They follow the energy. They are spontaneously themselves.

I feel at home in Italy. Wherever I go, whomever I meet, there is always a quality of the heart resonating in how we relate to each other. If you want to see this quality captured on film, I recommend a 1973 Italian movie called *Amarcord* by Federico Fellini, a comedy-drama about an adolescent boy growing up among an eccentric cast of characters in the village of Borgo San Giuliano. It portrays what I am talking about.

71

Another great movie, made twenty-four years later, was Roberto Benigni's *Life is Beautiful*, the story of a Jewish Italian shop owner who must employ his fertile imagination to shield his son from the horrors of internment in a Nazi concentration camp. Benigni shows how the heart quality can transform any situation.

At their best, Italians follow their intuition. For example, they put *so* much colour on the paper, then they step on the paper, destroy everything and start again. They don't care.

But, to be realistic, I need to say that this is only half the story – the best half. Like every nationality, Italians have two extremes. One is the heart. The other is a desire to control everything with the rational mind and insist on a logical explanation for everything. Naturally, I'm not referring to this side. I'm talking about a more essential Italian quality – one that allows people to enjoy spontaneity and chaos.

Undoing Social Training

I'm not saying all Italians know about spontaneity. In fact, when I begin my training there, I often say, "Even you Italians, you have to learn to be Italian!" And they start scratching their heads and wondering what I'm talking about, because many of them are not aware how deeply they've been conditioned and controlled – especially by Mama.

One thing I've discovered in Italy: God is nothing. The mother has much more power than God. Really, I mean it! The mother takes the *whole* authority of her children's lives upon herself, even after they have grown up.

I remember a scene from a well-known movie, *Big Blue*, in which one of the characters – a big, strong Italian man – was eating in a restaurant and his mother walked in and told him, "You are not allowed to eat in restaurants. You have to eat *my* food!"

Like everyone else, Italians have been corrupted by their social training. They've lost touch with their energy, their intuition. And when things get hard, like now, in this economic recession, they run home to Mama and Papa.

In a magazine I was reading recently, I learned that fifty percent of Italians aged 18-34 still live at home with their parents. When one government minister found out, he called for a new law forcing *bamboccioni* – or Mama's boys and girls – to leave the nest at 18.

By the way, through my use of Family Constellation as a therapeutic tool in my trainings, I have seen that a Mama's boy, or a Papa's daughter have little chance to enjoy a fulfilling relationship with a love partner. The pull from the original family is so strong that they lack the strength to create a new family system.

One young man told a newspaper that he was unemployed, staying at home, and he loved to cook. He wanted to help his parents by cooking meals for them, but his mother wouldn't hear of it! She couldn't imagine a situation in which a son can prepare a meal for his own Mama.

Living in the Heart

So, that's one side of their character. But what about the other side? When people ask me to explain myself, I tell them, "To be Italian means to live in the heart. Don't go with what the head is saying. Listen to the voice of your heart and take it with you into your painting."

This is absolutely necessary if you want to discover your own style of expression. If you want to find art that is original to you, then it needs to arise out of your own authentic creativity and for that you have to go past the head and into the heart.

Fortunately, it's not hard to seduce people into an 'Italian' mood, because this is an essential quality of the child in us. All I need to do is create a situation in which my participants can remember innocent playfulness. That's a reason why I invented the exercise of tearing up papers, which I use in Primal Painting. We dance, we play games, we splash paint in a carefree way and pretty soon, everyone gets the idea. From that moment onwards, it's not difficult to keep those qualities in our approach to painting.

Recently, during a visit to Istanbul, I went to see a theatre performance in a studio-theatre called 'The Garage'. On the stage, there was a red couch. That was all. As the performance began, a man came in and lay down on the couch and relaxed as if he was totally alone – just like we behave when nobody is around.

He started mumbling nonsense, as if he was bored with his life. He went on and on like that. Slowly, I became impatient, doubting why I had come. It seemed like a waste of time.

"Let's get out of here," I said to my companion and he agreed. As we stood up to leave, the man onstage suddenly took off his shirt. He had a great body. Then he gave a lion's roar. My mind stopped for a moment and I sat down again.

Then the man started singing like Pavarotti, the Italian opera singer, with no microphone and no music – just singing, naturally, by himself. It was so authentic and so touching that I felt glad we didn't leave the hall.

This simple theatre performance gave me an important message: how to be oneself, how to allow one's energy without compromising. Since then, whenever I facilitate a creative workshop, I think of that man.

"I Like it Like This"

Sometimes, students even outdo me. For example, one participant was a prominent professor at an Italian university. He came to the training for ten days and adopted an unusual method of painting. He placed the painting board across one knee and put his other knee on the floor. As you can imagine, the board wasn't level, or stable. It was always tipping this way or that, which meant that his colours were running off the board and dripping onto the floor all around him.

I asked him, "Can you please put your board on the floor, so that you don't make a big mess?"

He shrugged and replied, "Mi piace così!" ("I like it like this!") And he kept on painting like that. Well, I didn't feel like interfering any further, because this exchange happened during the 'Primal Painting' phase of my training. In this section, it's important to give people freedom to explore, because one of our biggest primal issues is over-control by our parents.

"My Masterpiece"

A few months later, this same professor came to the Mediterranean island of Ibiza to participate in my training there, which has a very different atmosphere and emphasis. On Ibiza, we paint elegantly in beautiful natural surroundings, in a forest near the sea. So, when I saw him, I thought, "Oh-oh, this is going to be a problem. He won't know how to paint in a beautiful way."

As if sensing my hesitation, the professor showed me a big, new, black portfolio and announced, "I will carry my masterpiece home in this folder."

I was watching him in the forest. Again, he was painting with the board on one knee and making a big mess. I had no hopes for his success. But on the last day, when the participants hung up their paintings, creating an exhibition in the forest, I noticed one painting that was so beautiful it nearly took my breath away. It belonged to the professor!

Allowing Negative Emotions

So, this is my teaching: to go where your mind is *not* guiding you. Don't worry if it seems weird or crazy. You need to experiment; focusing your awareness on impulses that come from a deeper place than your head.

One more thing about emotion: when you allow your feelings, they're not always going to be pretty. Negative emotions can also surface, and this is not a bad thing because they often create new and unusual elements in your painting.

For example, throwing anger onto a canvas in the form of a certain colour is going to look very different than if applied from the energy of love or happiness. The important thing is not to get stuck in anger, but to stay in tune with your energy, because energy is always moving, always changing.

Who's Afraid of Red?

I recall one woman from France who tended to be angry by nature. She was using only red paint on her canvas – red and red and red.

Experience has taught me how long to leave a person in this mood and sure enough, at a certain point, I sensed a turning point. She was stuck in her mood, I could see, but in a deeper way she was ready to go in a new direction.

So, I asked her, "If you close your eyes and tune into the energy of this moment, is there space for another colour that may want to be expressed?"

Immediately, she chose a sky blue. As she began to paint with this colour, I could also see a healing happening within her heart. This is a very important point: with sensitivity and experience, you can use painting for healing trauma because colours are deeply connected with our emotions and our unconscious patterns and memories.

Everything that is hidden inside us needs to be exposed and brought into the light of our conscious understanding. That's how healing happens. That's how we grow as painters, and as human beings.

Chapter Nine

Meditation Methods for Everyone

Osho says if you can jump into meditation totally, you don't need to do any therapy to develop your personal growth. With meditation, you are the therapist and the patient. You are working on yourself directly and you come to know your dignity as a conscious human being. Meditation is the basis of this journey of self-knowing. It is a commitment to explore oneself in order to be authentic, original, unique and real.

Many meditative techniques require us to sit still and be silent. But our modern lifestyle makes this difficult. Stress accumulates in the mind, tension accumulates in the body and so, before we can hope to access our inner silence and peace, we need to let go of all this tension and stress.

That's why Osho developed 'Active Meditations' in which there is an opportunity to unwind and release pent-up tension before trying to sit silently and be still.

Osho Dynamic Meditation

Osho created many different types of meditation, but Dynamic is probably the most important, as well as the most dramatic. It is one of the most unusual techniques ever developed and has become something of a hallmark of Osho's style.

When I facilitate Art Therapy workshops, it is inevitable that I will introduce Dynamic at some point, because to me it contains the answer to how to cope with the destructive nature of society and resurrect as an individual.

In this meditation, all human wisdom is somehow contained as a blueprint for a more conscious human being.

Dynamic lasts one hour and has five stages:

Stage One: The first stage is deep, fast, chaotic breathing, through the nose, emphasising the exhale. In a way, this is the most important stage of the meditation because if you do it right then the other four stages flow naturally and easily from it.

Sometimes I explain the first stage as 'baby breathing' because when a baby is born, when this new little being experiences the sudden shift from being cosy in mother's womb to having exposure to the big, wide world outside, the first thing he needs to do is take in a deep breath of air. He has never done it before. For nine months in the womb, he didn't need to breathe, but now, suddenly, in order to survive in this strange new world, the baby has to breathe with all his might – not just shallow breathing, but whole-body breathing. It is the only fitting response to beginning his life outside the womb.

This is how I encourage people to breathe...with totality. In a way, it is saying 'yes' to life. I also show them how to use body movement to help power the breathing method, so that by the time ten minutes have passed, a big charge of energy has built up inside the body and is ready to explode.

Stage Two: The second stage of Dynamic is catharsis. If the first stage has been done correctly it will put you in touch with your feelings and emotions. Then, without censoring or restricting yourself, you simply give expression to whatever wants to come out: anger, rage, tears, sadness, craziness, happiness...

The point is to give total permission to express whatever is there, emptying out your storehouse of emotions.

When you take a peek at a room full of meditators during the second stage of Dynamic, it looks and sounds like a madhouse. People are screaming, punching the air, rolling on the floor, stamping their feet, shouting at imaginary people, making all kinds of sounds.

The only rule is that you don't interfere with anyone else. This is your private, personal world, an opportunity to clean your mind of all kinds of crap and flush out any feelings that haven't had a chance to be vented.

Stage Three: After ten minutes, the third stage begins. It is very energetic: jumping up and down on the spot, with arms raised, shouting the mantra "Hoo! Hoo! Hoo!" As you can imagine, it is very challenging to do this for ten minutes, so I encourage people by saying things like: "You have come here to transform your life…well, this is the chance to do it. Now there's no way back, so keep going."

It is physically exhausting, and this is the point. By the time the first three stages of Dynamic are over, you have exhausted your mind, emotions and body. You are ready to stop, to be silent and to be still.

"Stop!"

Stage Four: The third stage is suddenly over and at the command "Stop!" people simply freeze in whatever position they find themselves. You freeze as if the whole world has stopped. No shifting position to be more comfortable, no scratching, no wiping away the sweat, no drink of water…just stop. In this fourth stage, which lasts 15 minutes, it is possible to taste meditation as a simple happening, arising out of non-doing, in which silence and stillness manifest spontaneously, and a sense of inner space grows by itself.

Stage Five: As the fourth stage ends, soft, slow, gentle music begins to play, gradually quickening in pace, and people dance to celebrate life, using whatever movements come naturally. This fifth and final stage lasts 15 minutes and then the meditation is over.

Kundalini Meditation

In the daily programme of meditations at the Osho Resort in Pune, Dynamic happens first thing in the morning, from 6-7 am, and Kundalini Meditation happens every evening, from 4:15-5:15 pm. Most Osho meditation centres around the world also keep to this schedule, using Dynamic as a morning wake-up call and Kundalini as the evening meditation to integrate, resolve and harmonise everything that has happened during the day.

Osho made it clear that, when leading any kind of workshop or training, these two meditations should be included in the daily programme, like two pillars supporting the rest of the work.

Kundalini Meditation is gentler than Dynamic, but is also active and vigorous in its approach. It lasts one hour and has four stages, each lasting 15 minutes.

Stage One: Shaking. We don't usually allow ourselves to shake. It doesn't look right and if other people are around we'd probably feel embarrassed. But, as a result, our bodies get stiff.

Osho says, "Whatever has life, shakes. Only the dead don't shake."

I tell people to stand with their legs shoulder-width apart so that the body is well supported and its various parts can be loose and relaxed...knees, pelvis, stomach, shoulders and so on. When the music starts, a little effort can be used to begin the shaking, but soon the shaking starts overtaking you, happening of its own accord.

Gradually, the whole body gets involved and it can be a very enjoyable experience.

Stage Two: Dancing. This is not about dance as a performance. It's not intended as an opportunity to show off your cool moves and, in any case, most people around you have their eyes closed and some will be wearing blindfolds to intensify their inner experience so there's usually nobody watching you. It's a spontaneous dance, formless, unplanned, in which the body follows the music in whatever way feels good.

Stage Three: Sitting or standing, listening to music. With the change in music, you stand still or sit comfortably. Once you have chosen your position, all movement should cease. You don't need to be stiff, but you should be quiet and still. All the energy that was going into outward expression through shaking and dancing now turns inward. Listening to music becomes a meditative experience.

Stage Four: Total relaxation. Participants lie down on the floor, on their backs, totally relaxed, simply letting the body go into rest. Sooner or later, we all have to learn how to die and most probably this will be the posture we will assume when leaving the body. In a way, meditation is a kind of death. Everything stops except the witnessing consciousness within us. Likewise, in Kundalini – everything ceases, but the inner awareness continues.

Other Meditations

Osho has devised many meditations, so I will not give a detailed description of each one because that will take a whole book in itself. Indeed, such a book already exists. It is called *Meditation: The First and Last Freedom*. It contains Osho's original meditation methods as well as other, more traditional techniques, that are also practised by his sannyasins.

Detailed descriptions of all of Osho's meditations can be found at www.osho.com. But here are the descriptions of some of the more popular meditation techniques we use on a daily or weekly basis. Unless otherwise stated, these meditations last for one hour.

Nataraj Meditation

Dance expressively, as if possessed, for 40 minutes, then lie down and be still for 20 minutes. The meditation ends with five minutes of dance celebration (65 minutes total).

Nadabrahma Meditation

Sit in a relaxed position with eyes closed and lips together, then start humming, loudly enough to be heard by others and create a vibration throughout your whole body. When the music changes, make slow outward circles with your hands, palms facing upward, then slow inward circles with palms facing down. In the final stage, sit silently and be still.

Devavani Meditation

Sit quietly, while music is playing, and then start making soft, gentle, nonsense sounds, for example: "la la la." These sounds arise from an unfamiliar part of the brain used as a child, before words were learned. Stand up and continue this unfamiliar language, allowing your body to move softly in harmony with the sound. Then lie down, be silent and still.

Gourishankar Meditation

Four stages of 15 minutes each. In the first stage, sit with closed eyes, inhaling deeply through the nose, filling the lungs. Hold the breath for as long as possible; then exhale gently through the mouth, then keep the lungs empty for as long as possible. Continue this breathing cycle throughout this stage. Osho says that if the breathing is done correctly in the first stage, the carbon dioxide gathering in the bloodstream will make you feel as high as Mount Gourishankar in the Himalayas. In the second stage, return to normal breathing and with a gentle gaze look at a candle flame or a flashing blue strobe light. Keep your body still. In the third stage, stand up and let your body move spontaneously, slowly and gently (this is 'latihan', which is explained under the Mahamudra Meditation below). In the fourth stage, lie down and be still.

Mandala Meditation

A powerful meditation that focuses your energy on the third eye. It has four stages, each lasting 15 minutes. In the first stage, with eyes open, run in place, bringing your knees up as high as possible and breathing deeply. In the second stage: sit with eyes closed, mouth open and let your body sway from the waist, like a reed blowing in the wind – from side to side, back and forth, around and around, as it happens. Third stage: lie on your back, keeping your head still. Open your eyes and rotate them in a clockwise direction. Sweep them fully around in the sockets as if you are following the second hand of a big clock. Start slowly, then gradually turn your eyes faster and faster. This brings your energy to the third eye. Final stage: close your eyes and be still.

Mahamudra Meditation

A method to connect yourself with the cosmos. Stand with closed eyes, allowing your body to be loose and receptive, waiting for subtle energies to arise spontaneously within the body and then cooperating with them. When you feel an impulse, start moving. Just allow it to happen. This is called *latihan*. In the second stage, kneel down with eyes closed, then raise both hands towards the sky, palms upward, your head like the mouth of an empty pot, your body hollow. Feel the energy filling you. Let it go as deeply as possible into your body, mind and soul. After two or three minutes, when you feel completely filled, bend forward and rest your forehead on the ground. Now pour the energy down into the earth. Take from the sky and give to the earth. Repeat this process at least seven times. Final stage: lie down and be still.

Guided Meditations

I learned how to use guided meditations from my colleague Sagarpriya and my partner Svagito – and, of course, from Osho himself, who frequently guided us into a meditative space at the end of his discourses.

A workshop facilitator or therapist can use guided meditations to take participants in any direction: into imaginary journeys, into meetings with parents, into conversations with higher aspects of oneself, into a deep experience of self-healing.

Any element can be used, but in all cases the effectiveness of the technique will depend on the inner space, or meditative quality, of the person transmitting the guidance. This is the determining factor. The method itself is secondary.

Chapter Ten

Family Constellation

To some people it may seem strange to include a chapter on Family Constellation in a book about Art Therapy. But it can't be helped. I am fascinated by the healing magic of this type of therapy. I have seen with my own eyes the benefits it can bring to a person's creative expression.

People work on personal issues through all kinds of therapeutic techniques. Some of these issues, like negative attitudes, self-criticism, lack of self-worth and so on, seem to stubbornly persist, despite our best efforts to change them. Here, Family Constellation can lend a hand, offering a different perspective on our personal problems.

As I explained earlier, Family Constellation offers us the opportunity to discover the burdens that children unintentionally take on, at a very early age, on behalf of members of previous generations in their families. When these burdens are recognised and given back, there is a big sense of relief and a release of tension, freeing the energy that was bound up in family drama.

Acknowledging All Family Members

How does Family Constellation work? Primarily with the understanding that every family member, whether good or bad, honest or dishonest, saint or sinner, needs to be acknowledged in his or her correct place within a single-family system. Correctness of place depends not on character or morality, but upon hierarchy and seniority.

All family members have the right to belong to the system, no matter what they may have done in their past.

If somebody was not acknowledged, or pushed out of the family, then later family members will be compelled to represent them – in a way to 'bring them back' – by becoming sick, taking on misery or suffering, acting in a certain way, and so on. Beneath the surface lies the need for everyone in this system to be loved and respected.

The roots of this immensely powerful need for recognition go back in human history to a time before the family unit, when the tribe was our only form of society. At that time, survival of the individual was impossible without the tribe, which was glued together by respect for the tribal elders and ancestors. Everyone had a fixed role.

To interfere with this structure was sure to create trouble for the tribe and that's how a collective psychology developed in which each person *had* to be acknowledged. Today, this tribal law is still locked deep inside us, within our collective unconscious.

In my work, I take a positive view of this ancient law. For example, if even one person had been missing in my family line, I would not be here. This understanding can be beneficial, because eventually you arrive at a feeling of gratitude towards everyone – not only in your own family tree but towards everyone who has ever walked on this planet.

In this context, I'd like to mention a Japanese movie called *Undertaker*. The Japanese title is *Okuribito*, which means, "the man who sends the dead to the other shore." It explores many of the themes raised by Hellinger's Family Constellation work. In Japan, on August 13th every year, all the ancestors are believed to come back to spend time with family members who are alive. At this time, one goes to the cemetery and places food, candles, incense and flowers on their graves.

The dead 'stay' for three days and then, on August 16th, they go back. On this day, one puts on a small boat, containing food and lit candles, on a river or in the ocean. In this way, the ancestors can return, satisfied and peacefully, to the other shore. In my experience, as someone with roots in Japan, if you do this with understanding it becomes an act of therapy.

You can expand this feeling of 'family' even wider, understanding that without the trees and the oceans and the animals, life would not be possible for us. Automatically, you become humble, loving and respectful.

The Parent-Child Connection

On a practical level, I focus on the impact that parents have on their children. As a reminder, within this relationship there are two basic movements: one is that, as a young child, you need to come really close to your parents; the other is that, as you grow up and become more mature, you need to grow away from them.

In the vast majority of people, neither of these movements is fully completed. As a result, many children, now adults, continue to be entangled with their parents, fighting with them, wanting somehow to be free of them, yet still preoccupied with them.

Bert Hellinger, the creator of this therapy, understands that we can't really separate from our parents unless we first bow down to them and thank them for all they have done for us. We may think that we can be free by rejecting and ignoring them, but trying to push them away is also a type of relationship. It is a negative bond that keeps parents and children tied to each other and can sometimes be even a stronger type of bondage than a positive, loving attitude.

With such a deep bonding, whatever you do to try and escape, the parents will haunt you.

The Gift of Life

It may seem hard to be grateful to parents who have, on the face of it, treated a child badly or harshly. But the sense of gratitude I'm talking about goes far deeper than superficial behaviour Essentially, it is gratitude for the gift of life.

Embracing this way of looking at ourselves is one of the biggest revolutions I can imagine because it is amazing how many of us simply take life for granted. We have no sense of the extraordinary gift of being alive, but instead busy ourselves with all kinds of distractions, often lapsing into a habit of complaining and creating misery for ourselves.

When you meditate, the experience of gratitude comes back to you. Why? Because meditation takes you into a deep awareness of the present moment. When past and future drop away, when only this present moment exists, when we are totally immersed in the 'here and now', there is an immediate understanding of how beautiful life is, of how nature surrounds us is in a continuous state of celebration and dance. In this state of gratitude, naturally, one's parents are included.

So, I don't adopt an exclusive attitude in my approach to Family Constellation. I'm not saying it is the only way to unburden oneself and learn how to live joyously. But Family Constellation and meditation work well together.

Why? Because Family Constellation work is essentially a process in which you learn to witness the constellation movements and dynamics unfolding in front of you, without judgement It is simply the case.

We were born in the context of a certain family system. We didn't make ourselves like that, nor did our parents. Everyone was just doing their best, while unknowingly creating burdens and unnecessary suffering for the next generation.

You can free yourself from these burdens by bringing a new understanding, by learning not to judge and by accepting yourself, by bowing down to your parents, by letting them go, and by focusing on the here and now. Then, you are no longer sandwiched between past and future.

Uncovering Family Secrets

In Family Constellation, everybody is to be acknowledged, even those who committed crimes, who went mad, who died very young, or who were somehow shut out of the family circle and concealed behind a veil of secrecy.

One of the wonders of Hellinger's work is how it succeeds in uncovering dark family secrets. There is a beauty about it because we see how attempts to smother the past or forget about unpleasant events, succeed only in creating burdens for future generations.

Everything needs to be exposed to the light of truth and understanding, so we can stop representing our older relatives and be free to be authentically ourselves. I am reminded of Osho's healing metaphor: unless you are willing to uncover your wounds and expose them in the light of understanding, healing is not possible.

Another relevant saying is that when an elephant passes by the door of your hut and the shadow of the elephant is cast on the floor, the elephant has already gone but the shadow remains. Don't cling to the shadow or be afraid of it – the elephant is no more.

In my personal experience, Osho's Dynamic Meditation is helpful in unburdening oneself of the past, emptying oneself of the old, standing in the present as an innocent child, open to the wonders of each moment as they unfold.

The Mysterious Morphogenic Field of Knowing

The way Family Constellation works is very mysterious. To function, it requires not only a client and therapist, but also a group of people who have agreed to act as representatives of the client's family members. The therapist invites the client to choose representatives – for the mother, father, grandmother, etc. – and place them in a constellation, or pattern.

As the representatives stand in their places within the constellation, they are able to feel the emotions, feelings, even the soul of those whom they represent. This work is amazing, not least because the representatives are often strangers who have no personal knowledge of the client's family history, and yet they are capable of accurately reflecting the emotions and attitudes of family members, whether living or dead.

Those who seek rational explanations say that every family, social group, tribe and nation on this planet creates what is called a 'morphogenic field' that binds all its members together. Nobody really knows what this field is, whether it is energy, thought-waves, electromagnetic imprints...all we can see are its effect, because after a short while the behaviour of the representatives begins to accurately mirror the dynamics of a client's family system and expose its secrets, burdens and destiny.

Of course, this cannot be scientifically proved, but anyone who experiences this work will see for themselves how remarkably accurate it can be.

However, I do need to mention that a good deal of training is needed before you can integrate Family Constellation into other types of work. You can't just take a participant's issue, pull a few people together in a constellation and hope something profound will come out of it. I participated in several of Bert Hellinger's workshops and spent many hours in Svagito's trainings before I felt skilled enough to do this work myself and to integrate it with Art Therapy. When I did combine the two, I found that the main benefit for people's creativity was to bring their psychology to the space of innocence. From this child-like space, the creative impulse can be felt, allowed and given its natural expression.

My own style of leading a Family Constellation session is spontaneous and simple: I simply welcome whatever is showing in the constellation. Imagine what life would be like if everybody can do this, dropping any grudge against past offenders, dropping judgement, putting aside any personal objections, saying 'yes' to life, and to your parents, with gratitude and love.

Exercise: Experiencing a Constellation

Having just stated that one needs training, I am going to contradict myself and invite you to experiment with constellation movements, even if you've had no prior experience, because even without skilled guidance you can, at least, have a taste of the basic work. Just remember to keep it simple.

To begin with, find two representatives and place your father and mother in front of you. The representatives don't need to know anything about your parents – their characters, what they did to you, etc.

You simply explore: how is it for you when your parents are standing in front of you. What emotions, what feelings, what thoughts do their presence trigger in you?

After a while, you can invite the people in the constellation to move, following any bodily sensations or impulses. Soon, this simple constellation will begin to reflect what's happening in the dynamic of your relationship with your parents. Watch, without judgement, as the reality of your relationship begins to be revealed.

Working with a single partner, you can explore the dynamic between yourself and your mother. You become your mother, while your partner becomes you. Stand in a constellation and then allow the movement to unfold for about ten minutes.

Through this very simple structure, you can begin to understand your mother's position. How is it, to be your mother standing in front of her child? What feelings arise in her and what kind of burden is she carrying? Just a simple constellation like this can be a powerful experience as you begin to sense your mother's life patterns.

Blocking Creative Flow

Let's look at the case of Suzie, a Chinese woman from Hong Kong in her early forties, who participated in one of my trainings. During an exercise in partner painting, she became aware of a difficulty that was blocking her creativity.

In a sharing session, she told the group, "Since I was a child, I have had a huge, cold wall on my back. My mother was always whacking me with something from behind. So now, whenever the desire to be creative starts to happen, I feel this frozen sensation in my back."

Suzie had already found a partial solution to her difficulty, thanks to her painting partner, a big, motherly Russian woman called Alexandra.

"As I was painting, Alexandra sat behind me and put her hand on my back. She was stroking me with her hand, which felt warm, soft and loving. I knew I could trust her – she wasn't going to whack me. After a while, I noticed my defensive wall melting and I could allow her love to enter me. For the first time, I sensed what love is."

I reminded Suzie that the effect of Alexandra's loving presence could not have happened if her own love, which she carries inside herself, had not been activated. Then she got a shock, because I added, "This is also your mother's love for you that you are feeling."

I explained, "Your mother could have chosen to have an abortion. But she didn't do that. She didn't decide to finish you. That's why you're here. So, even though you carry the pain of her beating, this experience is also a reminder of your mother's love."

As a way of healing her wound, I suggested, "Whenever the frozen feeling comes into your back, remember Alexandra's hand, the sensation of her love flowing into your back, and then just say 'thank you' to your mother."

This was a breakthrough moment for Suzie. Even before she put my suggestion into practice, she got the point and her creative block began to dissolve.

A word here about personal problems and issues: one is tempted to think that "If I had no obstacles or problems in my life, I would be stronger and healthier." But, sometimes it is precisely because of one's difficulties that one gains a certain strength, which would not have necessarily happened in an easier life.

The Burden of Responsibility

Gratitude is a healing and freeing force. Bowing down to our parents allows us to move away from them. For the first time, we can be truly free of the powerful grip that a family member can exert on us.

I have no fixed plan when conducting a training. But one thing I know for sure: when we dive into the process, all kinds of psychological issues start to surface in the participants. Many of these difficulties inhibit a person's ability to allow a natural flow of creative expression.

Peggy is an accomplished artist from Australia and creates excellent portraits, but there's a darkness, or heaviness, surrounding her work. I get the feeling that she's carrying a huge burden on her shoulders and this weighs down her spirit. She's a really good painter, but not connected with her joy - and I can certainly understand why. She has two sisters who are mentally handicapped and a mother and father who are in continuous conflict with one another.

In this stressful situation, Peggy runs between them all, trying to keep her family together and hoping to create a stable and harmonious situation for everyone. Her self-image is that she's playing a very important role, organising everybody and making peace. But, really, as we shall see, it's not her job.

Finding Her True Place

We set up Peggy's constellation and soon it becomes clear that there are many issues within her family system. We discover that two of Peggy's siblings died in childbirth, but she also has two living brothers who are ready to be a source of nourishment and support for her.

The moment of truth comes when Peggy allows herself to be held by her brothers and, from this safe and supported space, looks at her mother. Her mother, seeing the children standing together with love for each other, can also relax.

This is the moment for Peggy to speak to her mother, using key statements developed by Hellinger, such as: "I am small, you are big" and "You give and I receive." This makes it clear that it's not Peggy's job to organise the family. It's not her responsibility to make everyone happy. Looking around at the other family members, she can say, "I am the fifth child. I'm just one of you."

Peggy can now approach her mother, stand in front of her and tell her that she will no longer carry pain and guilt on her behalf. "I honour your pain. I give it back to you and I leave you to your destiny," she says in a voice filled with love and understanding.

Family Constellation is known as a "single intervention" therapy, because usually only one session is needed for each issue. Once a session is over, the Constellation Therapist withdraws from involvement with a "patient" and allows the new understanding to do its work. Change occurs alchemically, organically, by itself. The correct order – also known as the "sacred order" – is recognised and restored within the family system. These changes not only affect the client, but often influence other family members, as well, as the order becomes restored.

Transforming Effect

Perhaps the most touching aspect of Family Constellation is the willingness with which small children take on the burdens of their parents and other senior relatives out of their love for them.

This arises out of a child-like, magical belief that we can somehow alleviate the suffering of others by taking it over, putting the burden on ourselves. But this love is misguided and self-destructive.

Taking on the burdens of others will cripple the child's individuality, until such time as those burdens are understood and given back.

Effect on Creativity

As I've already indicated, my special interest in Family Constellation is the transforming effect it can have on people's creative expression. Essentially, I'm inviting participants to move towards a free, uninhibited flow of energy that can find expression spontaneously, in the moment, without being suppressed, held back, or diverted.

As the burdens carried from childhood are recognised and dissolved, this process gets easier and easier. We're all looking for that innocent, playful and endless fountain of creative energy that we had when we were young. Family Constellation gives a helping hand toward that end.

For example, I sometimes combine Family Constellation Therapy with painting one's own self-portrait. As you can imagine, working with one's parents and absorbing lessons from a constellation can offer many insights into one's own nature. This is sure to be reflected in the self-portrait.

Recently, I was invited by the Korean Art Therapy Association to facilitate a workshop for 240 therapists in Keishiyu, South Korea. I shared my understanding of Family Constellation and opened a constellation with them to demonstrate its effect.

Many people were deeply moved and in this way started looking at one of the most basic issues in therapy: the relationship to one's parents.

Each country has a different type of conditioning and social background, but every human being has parents, has roots in the family system, and has the same longing to be loved and to love others.

Chapter Eleven

Painting Your Dance

Sometimes I start a group with an exercise called 'Dancing Your Name'. The purpose is to get in touch with one's own natural expression. It's not an intellectual concept or preconceived idea about 'who I am'; we already have so many ideas about that, usually reflecting other people's opinions about us. It's more like exploring the question, "What is my quality? Can I show how I'm feeling right now, through dancing?" It's a valuable way to discover another, hidden voice inside us.

This exercise can be done with or without music. It's interesting to explore the movement between the two – between sound and silence. Everybody has a tendency to dance when music is on and then stop when it is turned off, so I invite people to keep on dancing without music, just to capture a new flavour.

Here, I introduce an understanding about intimacy. Intimacy doesn't need time. Intimacy has something to do with one's state of being. When you are open, truthful and available to another person it immediately becomes infectious. The other cannot resist opening up to you. Intimacy doesn't require people to 'get to know each other' over a period of weeks, months or years. In fact, some people can relate over long periods and never really get to know each other. Dancing one's name, sharing one's energy without words, is a good beginning to establish an intimate connection in a very short period of time.

Child-Like and Childishness

Dance often carries the playful quality of children so perhaps I should say more about the psychological state I refer to as 'the child'. Naturally, when we were children, there was so much we didn't know and needed to learn.

As adults, we can also be childish in our behaviour, which can simply mean that we are being a little bit stupid. There's a big difference between being 'childish' and being 'child-like'. When we are child-like, our behaviour and attitudes carry the qualities of innocence and freshness without any childishness.

In this state of regained innocence, you can discover your originality. If you can awaken this state inside yourself – I should really say 'reawaken' because it has never been lost – you can become aware that you have something to say, you have something to offer, you have something to contribute in this lifetime.

The Dance Inside Us

In the *Painting Your Dance* workshops, we take a close look at our relationship with our bodies. We ask ourselves questions like: "Do I respect my body? Do I listen to my body? Can I sense the life force pulsing through it? Can I give expression to the energy that arises within its form? Can I dance with my body, flow with my body, enjoy its movements?"

This approach helps people understand the importance of allowing personal expression in their daily lives. Life is a continuous flow of movement and expression, but people tend to hold back, often monitoring and censoring their response to life, not listening to their own inner impulses, afraid that spontaneous expression may be condemned by others.

For example, in one sharing during a *Painting Your Dance* workshop, a Chinese woman thanked me for bringing more vitality into her life. So, as a challenge, I invited her to come into the middle of our sharing circle and allow any spontaneous movement to course through her body.

For a few seconds she was hesitant, but then suddenly she got up, went to the middle of the circle, opened her arms wide, looked up to the sky, and then lay down on the floor like a star, with legs and arms spread wide, like Leonardo da Vinci's famous drawing.

Then I asked the group, "When somebody takes a jump and expresses her energy in action, do you want to remain a spectator, or do you wish to join her?"

Immediately, several people got up, laid down in the middle of the circle and added to the Chinese woman's star, connecting hands or feet, arms or legs, spreading out through the room. Soon, they were joined by others until finally about 50 people covered the whole floor, all connected with each other.

This is one of the aims of this section: to help people understand that nobody is an island. We are part of one big human continent. Even what appears to be a solitary island out in the ocean is actually connected with the land beneath the sea. So, in a group like this, whatever an individual is going through, the other participants are bound to be affected.

When words are not in the way, it is easier to enter into another's being or heart, and the body language of dance is particularly helpful, because in dancing together we are becoming aware of the distance between people, the closeness, the shared movements, the eye contact...all of these elements contribute to authentic expression.

Here, I want to talk about authentic performance. Having a passion for dance myself, I would like to share the story of a dance performance I arranged in one of the biggest bookshops in Tokyo. I was invited to give a talk with four slide projectors projecting my paintings on a large screen. In front, I intended to dance, wearing a white dress and using other white cloth.

Ten minutes before the show, the manager asked me, "Aren't you going to rehearse before the show?"

"I have never rehearsed anything in my life," I replied.

He was surprised, and worried. "You are not going to talk about your guru and his religion, I hope?"

"If you don't trust me, I can just go home," I answered. But the audience was already there, so he hurriedly said, "Just stay and do whatever you like."

Then I came out on the stage. All the spotlights were on me, so the audience was in absolute darkness. I couldn't see anyone, but, of course, I knew they were all silently watching and waiting.

I got frightened. My knees start shaking. So, I said to the audience, "Look! My knees are shaking! I can't stand any longer, I have to sit down."

I sat down in the lotus posture. Osho entered into my being and I became calm, so I talked about him and what I learned from him. Then the energy came back into my body and I danced in front of the screen, allowing all the colours of my paintings to be projected on my body and onto the sheets of moving white cloth. It was an amazing experience and the audience loved it.

The challenge of performance provokes all kinds of issues, such as fear of being embarrassed or exposed in front of the audience. But it is a healthy challenge. It is helpful to work with people that can help you face all kinds of hidden fears.

For example, in a certain sense, one has to perform in front of an audience in order to lead a workshop.

Usually, one thinks that talent, training, discipline and practice are needed for a dance performance. And, of course, for a ballet performance or a TV dance show, this is certainly true.

But there are other approaches worth exploring. If you know how to click into your own energy and to naturally express that energy, this can serve as a message in itself. I don't mean to dismiss the benefits of training, but connecting with your own essential core will transform any dance expression, instilling both a sense of self-trust and confidence.

The key point is spontaneity – allowing expression without mental calculation. A great healing happens. Suddenly, you feel like saying, "Yes, I am alive! Yes, I have something to offer to myself and to others. I have a song to sing. I have a dance inside me that wants to come out."

To reconnect with this state is important if we are to experience fulfilment as artists. And for this reconnection to happen, dance is a must. It is a key that unlocks the doors of creativity.

Ever since I can remember, I've been aware of the transforming quality of dance. My mother wanted to be a dancer, but she couldn't manage it, because it was wartime in Japan. But I remember one time, in a small village theatre near our home, my mother and her younger sister gave a dance performance on stage.

I don't know how others saw their dancing, but I experienced it as magical. Suddenly, the mother whom I thought I knew, simply disappeared. I think you must know the mother I mean, because mothers are universal. They are always worrying about their children, training them, educating them, feeding them, washing them, so naturally, the child sees the mother in this way.

But when my mother appeared on stage and began to dance, the whole imprint disappeared, and I saw this beautiful, elegant woman expressing something of herself I'd never seen her express before. I never even imagined that such a state existed.

The Dancer and the Dance

I carry the same longing for dance as she did, and happily my parents decided to send me to dance classes from the age of five onwards. One of the first things I learned was that dance doesn't exist separately from the dancer. It's not like a painting. It's not an object. When you are a dancer, the dance exists, but only for that time. When you stop, the dance disappears.

Later on, I understood that life also has this quality. When you say 'yes' to life and participate with energy and enthusiasm, you are able to feel alive – to feel the pulse of life, within and without. It's only when you choose *not* to say 'yes' that life becomes dull. Literally, you become 'lifeless'.

Dance has many aspects. As I mentioned in the section about African dance, my early teachers emphasised the importance of placing one's awareness not only in the feet and legs, but also in the back, which I found intriguing. Normally, we are preoccupied with the front of our bodies, because this is what we show when we relate with others.

Just think about it for a moment. We don't usually say 'hello' or carry on a conversation with our backs turned, so we don't pay much attention to this area. But in dance it gives you depth, poise and presence that can otherwise be difficult to experience.

Learning Awareness through Calligraphy

Another surprising lesson in my dance studies was an association with qualities that are taught in the traditional art of calligraphy. For example, in calligraphy, you learn about your centre of gravity, your *hara*; you learn to be aware of your body, your breathing and the right moment to say 'yes' and connect your brush with the blank sheet of paper in front of you.

Basically, by doing calligraphy, you tune into the here and now. It is yet another method for attaining a 'No Mind' space. You learn to be aware of your inner emptiness, letting your mind become unoccupied so existence can sing a song through you. It is, in itself, a kind of dance, an expression of energy that begins deep inside and manifests as a flowing movement of black ink on white paper.

As I talk about the dance of calligraphy, I feel compelled to also mention the Sufi tradition of whirling. Here, the whole world is turning but your centre is still and unmoving. I invited a Russian friend of mine, Ida, to dance while I taught calligraphy because she exhibits a certain natural quality. Although she dances with intense speed and movement, her centre is always still and relaxed.

To bring this understanding into one's life is a valuable pursuit. We tend to choose either action or inaction; not realising that each complements the other. Calligraphy deals with the harmony that is hidden in the flow between opposites: black and white, day and night, darkness and light, form and no-form, doing and non-doing.

Calligraphy instils a basic truth: the beauty of a few brush strokes doesn't depend only on technique, but on the inner state of the calligrapher. The more he can empty himself, the more he can relax and become a hollow bamboo, the more he will be able to act as a vehicle for something beyond himself and the more he will access something of the mysterious, or the Divine.

As a child, to celebrate the Japanese New Year, black ink and brushes were set out in my parents' house for a calligraphy event. Before anyone arrived, I felt a sudden impulse; I picked up a brush, dipped it in black ink, and decorated all the white paper sliding doors in the house! It felt so good! Although I was punished for it, the good feeling never left me. It is with me still, reminding me of the importance to connect the black ink with the energy of the inner dance. It is magic to allow hands to dance through calligraphy.

This reminds me of an ancient Japanese story of an emperor who ordered his calligrapher to create one simple symbol for him. The calligrapher agreed, demanded a huge sum of money, then disappeared from the court.

Nothing was heard of him for three years. Then, he suddenly reappeared at the court, bowed before the king, laid out his pens, brushes, and papers, and took just a mere moment to draw a symbol.

The emperor was not displeased by this apparently puzzling behaviour. He understood that the calligrapher needed three years to prepare himself internally for the apparently simple task he'd given him.

Here, I would like to say something about Osho's signatures, which inspired me. I first saw them in the 1970s, when he was signing his name, 'Bhagwan Shree Rajneesh'. I couldn't believe how perfect his signature was; how relaxed, how creative, how absolutely in the here and now it appeared.

Whatever is touched by an enlightened being, his expression gives a unique message that can take a disciple into a space of meditation. One simply becomes silent and is drawn to a higher level of consciousness.

When initiating people into 'neo-sannyas', or disciplehood, he would write their name on a piece of paper and then sign underneath. I was intrigued how he held the pen – the same way we learned to hold a brush for calligraphy: the brush standing straight, supported by two fingers in front and two behind.

Osho once said that, to him, every moment is perfect in itself, in its imperfection. For example, even though he was giving a discourse every morning for 90 minutes or more, it would have been okay with him to leave any sentence or paragraph incomplete, just in the middle, because he had no particular intended goal other than what was being conveyed each moment by his presence.

His approach is just the opposite of traditional speech delivery, which focuses the speaker to make sure that the speech is well-researched, perfectly delivered, follows a rational line of argument to a logical conclusion...and so on. Bringing this fresh perspective into other areas of one's own life provides opportunities for a totally different way of being in the world.

Relaxed & Effortless

Here is how I recommend you prepare for a calligraphy session. You sit comfortably in a meditative posture, checking your body for any tension. An awareness of the body, checking in this way, takes you naturally into a state of relaxation. When the mind is quiet, when you can feel and hear your heart, you are ready to apply the brush to the paper. The action of the brush arises from this meditative space.

The most important thing is: when you begin your movement, you do not hesitate or try to stop or change the flow. Once you start, there is no way to go back – that's the beauty of calligraphy. There is no question of second thoughts or attempts to correct what has appeared on the paper.

Through this, one learns how to move forward in life without looking back. Each step of calligraphy is connected with an inner dance of energy and awareness.

I remember, when I was painting illustrations for Osho's books, there was a series on Zen Master Dogen, which Osho had dedicated to the full moon. So, of course, I had to paint the full moon. I tried this way and that, but nothing satisfied me.

Then I realised: the full moon is not the outer object, floating in the sky, but a metaphor for one's own inner fullness. Once I understood this, my way of painting the moon changed. It became more like calligraphy...just being in my centre, going with the energy, allowing the moon to appear on the painting.

When I talk to my participants about nature painting, I mention this aspect of calligraphy and illustrate the point by explaining how students of this art are trained. The master stands behind the student, taking his hands, moving them as the characters are drawn. In this way, the student has an experience of the relaxed effortlessness that makes for a good artist.

It's a dance without tension, without intention, without mind. The master is dancing with the student. When I look at the dance of nature, it is the same. Nature is vital, dynamic and yet utterly relaxed. This is what makes for its perfection.

If I'm going to paint a tree, I need to acquire some insight into how trees express themselves.

"Why are they so beautiful? Why are they so perfect? How does it feel to be in harmony with the tree's quality of dancing with existence?"

It's something I discovered for myself, but, of course, I'm not the only one to have done so. If you happen to be visiting San Francisco, you can take a short drive north to Muir Woods, named after John Muir □ the famous Scottish-born American naturalist and early advocate of preservation of wilderness areas in the United States □ to experience what he wrote about.

Muir was an environmentalist way back in the nineteenth century, when such people were considered enemies of economic development. He took plenty of risks in his quest for understanding the natural beauty around him.

It is said that during wild stormy weather he would climb tall pine trees, or redwoods, bind himself to the trunk with a rope and for hours enjoy the dance of the tree in the wind. Muir is my kind of guy – a little crazy and yet with a deep understanding of the ecstasy of nature.

There is a similar story in the Zen tradition. One day, a disciple came to his master and showed him a painting of bamboo. The master hit him saying, "You don't know how to paint! Go to the bamboo grove, sit there and learn from the bamboo. Unless you become the bamboo yourself, don't come back!"

Days passed, then weeks, then months. The master became worried and went to look for the disciple. He found him standing, with eyes closed, in the middle of a bamboo forest, swaying in the wind, just like the bamboo around him. The master had to shake him and say, "Enough! Come back and start painting!"

It is my wish for everyone to learn this method of accessing and expressing creativity.

Your personal expansion takes priority, then comes the painting. Whatever arises out of your expansiveness will be beautiful.

Pulling Out Weeds

Once you understand that dance is a natural expression of human energy, you are ready to learn something important about your conditioning. You start to wonder what is blocking or preventing this dance from manifesting in your life. This is one of the reasons people become interested in therapy. They realise that they've been blocked, and they want to be free.

Therapy is like pulling weeds out of the ground so that a rose bush and other flowers can grow. You learn how to dig through the weeds within yourself so that your pain, your problems, your hidden darkness no longer choke out the roots of your creativity.

Dance as Therapy

Without identifying a specific issue, without reliving a childhood trauma and without any fuss, the joy of dancing can heal people, all by itself.

For example, in the *Painting Your Dance* workshop, we begin by dancing in the open air. Under a canopy of trees, with the morning sunlight entering through the leaves, on a warm spring day, we have a beautiful and natural environment in which to explore movement and music.

I lead the group in simple movements at first, slowly opening the hands and arms in a gesture of expansion. This is a good way to start because with this simple gesture, I'm inviting people to open up and explore beyond their normal boundaries.

Exercises like Dancing your Name, mirroring each other's movements, flowing like seaweed...these are all ways of warming up, sharing energy, seducing people into a sense of openness and creativity.

Another favourite of mine is suggesting to people that all of their fingers have become paint brushes, filled with different colours, so that rainbow colours are pouring out of them.

With this image in mind, they begin to paint each other with imaginary colours. It is a joyous sight to observe, because everyone becomes a beautiful, radiant being. To be painted and sculpted with rainbow colours is a gift for one's heart, washing away old judgements about oneself. The exercise has a double effect: feeling beautiful yourself and also making someone else feel beautiful through your creativity.

Energy Ball Exercise

The Energy Ball is effective for exploring communication, imagination and dance all at the same time. It was created by a good friend of mine, Navanita, who is an experienced dance therapist.

"Choose a partner and stand in front of each other," I instruct the group. "Close your eyes and place your hands gently on your belly. Now imagine that your belly contains an energy ball."

While guiding people into an exercise like this, it's important to encourage them to use their sensitivity, tuning into their feelings to create a clear image of a ball beneath their hands.

"How big is the energy ball in your belly?" I ask. "What colour is it? What size? Is it watery, rubbery or solid? What temperature does it have? Is it heavy or light? Is the texture velvety, smooth, or rough?"

I give them plenty of time to form an image, then ask them to open their eyes and decide who is Partner A and who is Partner B.

"Partner A, take your energy ball out of your belly and show it to your partner. Without words, try to convey its size, weight, texture and what feelings and emotions it may contain."

The emotional content is important. This will help these participants become familiar with the concept that feelings are also energy and evoke awareness of emotions that may be hidden in the body. The ball may be happy, sad, angry □ any kind of emotion is allowed.

"Okay, now you are going to play with your ball," I guide them. "Use your whole body. Find out how you want to play with your ball and then include your partner in that play."

It's a nice way to introduce dance. As you pass the ball back and forth, receiving it in your hands, your body movement starts changing and adapting. And it's a playful atmosphere with lots of space available under our tree canopy. Pretty soon, partners are running around the open space. Some are throwing the ball to each other, some are pushing it and others are rolling it.

Loosening the Grip of Emotions

One of the reasons why we get stuck, as energy beings, is that we identify with our emotions. They take hold of us and seem difficult to shake off. But when we consciously take them out and start fooling around with them, the grip of identification is bound to loosen up and our energy automatically starts to expand.

"Watch the way how your ball starts changing its shape, weight, colour or size as you play together," I suggest, to support the process of loosening up.

When the game has gone on long enough, I ring a bell and ask them to switch over. Partner A puts his energy ball back in his stomach and Partner B brings his energy ball out and describes it to his partner.

A Revolutionary Step

I invite people to choose a painting partner. Two pieces of paper are placed vertically next to each other, with paints and water in between. One partner dances, while the other is painting. The one who is painting looks mainly at the one who is dancing. As he does so, he is painting, but pays little attention to the shapes and colours that are finding expression on the paper. The essential thing is to be in tune with the dancer and to allow this 'in tune-ness' to move through the brush onto the paper.

Then the two partners change roles and begin again.

Another, similar approach is to see the movement of one's own hand and brush as a dance. Here, I encourage participants to forget that it's a painting, but simply to focus on the feeling of allowing the paint brush to dance on the paper, regardless of what is finding expression.

As you can see, dance as therapy is very different from normal social dancing in which people are performing rehearsed routines, while smoking, chatting, drinking... anything but focusing on the dance itself. To bring full awareness into one's own body and actually experience the dance can be a revolutionary experience of embodiment for many adults.

In my workshops, we focus on dance first and then, when I feel the participants are ready, bring this energy to the brushes and paper. It is only then that we can give expression to the energy we have tapped into through our paint brushes.

Dance comes first for many reasons. In dance you are less concerned with the outcome of your creativity. Dancers don't stay in one fixed pose, but are continuously moving and this element can be transferred to the way that you paint. With this understanding, it's easier to let go of fixed ideas or particular forms and to access the joys of becoming more spontaneous.

When people begin to enjoy painting through dance, it is already a success because they are saying 'yes' to their energy. Once they say 'yes' to their energy, anything can happen. The doors of creativity are wide open.

Another exercise I enjoy is to invite participants to form a big circle, standing next to each other in a relaxed and easy fashion while dancing to the music. One person comes into the centre of the circle and dances alone, not as a performance but as a natural expression of his or her present energy. The others copy the movement and style of the one in the middle. After a minute or two, the person in the middle comes back to the circumference of the circle and chooses the next person, who enters the centre. In this way, people learn a variety of dance expressions from a wide variety of individuals.

My love affair with dance pervades the whole Art Therapy Training. At the end of the training we will create a public performance in which all the participants, helpers and assistants will dance for the public.

To take part in the performance can be quite therapeutic because you examine your sense of self-worth as well of any fear you might have of exhibiting yourself before others. When the performance is a well-received success – as it always is – a new sense of self-respect is instilled. The realisation that "Yes, I have something to offer to others. I have a message worth delivering," can be truly life-changing.

One of the most thrilling and beautiful performances that we create utilises photos of our paintings in the form of colour slides. These are projected onto several screens before we come dancing onto the stage between the screens and the projector, dressed in white clothes and carrying white scarves and large pieces of white cloth. The colourful images from the slides are projected on our movements, creating a wonderful, ever-changing, ever-flowing, dancing river of colour. It is a synthesis of painting, dance and theatre.

To dance in a group is to allow yourself to disappear into others, experiencing that you are not an island, that you are an integral part of existence. And the most essential discovery of all is to learn that you will still be you, even when you are part of a Whole.

If you become aware of the immense transformative capacity of dance, you can apply this insight into your life, regardless of what you do. When people integrate dance with painting, they become less attached to the outcome of their creativity. Dancers don't cling to a static formation; they are continuously moving. This flexible element can be transferred from dance to the way people paint and, with this understanding, it's easier for them to let go of stagnation.

When people begin to enjoy painting through dance, they say 'yes' to their energy. And once they say 'yes' to their energy, anything can happen. The doors of creativity open wide.

Chapter Twelve

Group Dynamics

By now you will have understood that I like working with the collective energy of a large group of people. When exploring painting together, people not only learn about their own qualities, but also experience the wide spectrum of expression that others bring to a project. Each member of the group has something unique to share, and learning how to respect each other's qualities is a delicate art.

I provide participants with big canvases. They are really big – about the size of four single mattresses formed into a square. Five people work on one canvas, using acrylic paints and inks. In my current training, there are eight groups in all, totalling 40 people.

The advantage of using canvas is that it doesn't break easily. You can pour layers of paint on it, soak it, sponge it, scrub it off, start again...even dance on it. Canvas is much stronger than paper, so for a group exercise, canvas provides big advantages.

The first time we move into this exercise, I allow people to form their own groups, choosing whom they want to work with, inviting them to look at each other through the perspective of energy rather than personality.

"Which energies do you want to work with today?" I inquire.

Clear Boundaries

Once the groups are formed, I invite them to divide up the canvas into five equal sections, so that each person gets the same amount of territory. This is the easiest way to start because it helps people to relax.

With boundaries already defined, they are not so nervous about protecting their space or fearful about being imposed upon by others.

A riskier way to begin the exercise is to invite people to decide for themselves how much space they need and draw their own territorial lines on the paper. According to their nature, some will easily and quickly claim a generous amount of space, while others will shyly wait until the end to see how much space is left for them. Or, another option is for the facilitator to let everyone begin to paint at the same time without dividing the paper into sections.

However, I have chosen the first approach, equally dividing up the paper, and my participants begin to paint on their own section of canvas. After about half-an-hour I say, "Stop!" We will be stopping and starting many times because when the colours are flowing and the music is pumping, each group's dynamics are moving too fast to maintain a true perspective on what is actually happening. When everything stops, when no one is doing anything, we can all begin to see more clearly.

I invite participants to look at all five sections of the painting and take turns to explain the quality they have been manifesting. For example, one painter might say, "My quality is harmony," while another may say, "My quality is sensitivity," and so on.

Recognising Beauty

I also introduce an appreciation for beauty in a way that invites people to speak out and stand up for their own ideas about beauty, while at the same time opening up to the ideas of others.

"Each member of the group has to speak up. Show the others where you see beauty in what you have done," I prompt. "You need to tell them clearly, 'This is beautiful and I don't want it to be disturbed. Please respect this.'"

In this way, each person's sensibility for beauty grows and expands. It happens in two ways: first, you have to recognise and stand for the beauty in your own painting, in what you, yourself have created. Second, you become more open to other people's ideas about beauty, which may be totally different from your own.

As the painting continues, boundaries between the participants merge and overlap. Sometimes, this is a harmonious experience. If so, participants can enjoy the sweet intimacy of working together like an orchestra, with different musicians playing harmoniously, creating a symphony as the five separate paintings slowly become one.

Speaking Up

Often, however, there is conflict and I am not one to shy away from it. Rather, I open the subject up for discussion. During one of the many pauses in the process, I ask the participants to look around and check, "Who is getting more space? Who feels cramped? Who thinks that their individual contribution is being disrespected, or perhaps even destroyed? Now is to the time to speak up!"

Inevitably, there are people who feel they have been invaded, over-ridden, and this is the moment when they must have the courage to say so. Often, it's those people whose nature is to remain silent and suffer who must now take a deep breath, speak out, and stand up for themselves.

Communication in these situations is a delicate affair. If you don't speak out, you can't communicate with your partners. If you do speak out, then often what you say carries an emotional charge if you have become too identified with your painting. This charge is likely to cause other people to react. Someone may become angry or defensive, hindering communication in a new and different way.

Emotional Crisis

Sure enough, emotional crises often develop between two participants. In one instance, one of the participants was a German woman from Munich, called Birgit. The other was an American woman from Dallas, Texas called Barbara. Both were in their forties.

Barbara felt that Birgit had invaded her territory on the canvas and was really upset. "I feel powerless to defend myself," she confessed. Her energy collapsed as she cried.

I decided to work with Birgit, because Barbara wasn't able to see anything clearly in her present emotional state. Although, later, once she had calmed down, she would have. Because Birgit was so strong, so self-assured, I intuitively felt that, at that moment, the Star Sapphire therapy developed by Sagarpriya DeLong Miller was the right tool to use with her. It was obvious that she was tapped into her male energy and that's probably why Barbara felt so weak and helpless.

Exploring the Male-Female Polarity

There is a simple and effective way to connect people with their male and female polarities.

We work with the basic understanding that the right side of the body is male, the left side is female. So, when I asked Birgit to close her right eye and look at me through her left eye while talking to me, I invited her feminine side to address me.

By the way, this can be a useful key: whenever you have a problem and feel stuck, it can be effective to look at the issue through different eyes, seeing how each polarity inside us relates to the challenge. These polarities are in-built and true for everyone. We are born out of the union between a man and a woman – our father and mother – and so it is natural that we have these two qualities inside us.

With Birgit, the dynamics of the external conflict were soon exposed, because her internal feminine side was a mirror image of Barbara. Her inner woman told me that she felt unacknowledged, unlived, unwelcomed. In everyday life, it had been Birgit's male side that was running the show, making all the decisions, doing all the work, taking as much space as 'he' needs.

Birgit was an intelligent woman, open to exploring her inner world, so she was able to recognise that the quality she had been rejecting in Barbara was also being rejected within her own psyche.

Nourishing the Inner Woman

With this foundation of understanding, my direction was clear. I needed to take time to listen to Birgit's inner woman, providing the safe space she needed to come out and express herself. I listened to her and let her know that she was being heard. To support her, I asked Birgit to place both hands on her own heart and bring her attention to that area, breathing softly and slowly into her heart.

This helped her to soften and relax; to let down her defences.

In this way, her inner woman felt nourished and that's really all that was needed. I didn't deal with the outer conflict. I simply revealed Birgit's inner reality and suggested the possibility that she may like to connect with her inner woman more often, taking time to listen to her; understanding that softness, gentleness and vulnerability are not a sign of weakness; they are qualities to be valued and cherished, especially in a woman.

Tuning In

The next day, I presented the group with new white canvases and chose eight experienced painters, to each stand by a canvas. Then I invited the participants to choose which painter they would like to join.

Once again, this was an opportunity for people to check in within themselves and tune into their own energy, then look around and see which of the eight experienced painters is best suited to them. I want people to learn this knack of checking inside before moving into action. So often we simply move out of habit, or react to superficial impulses, without regard to our inner feelings.

When everyone is settled, I explained that the experienced painters would demonstrate a way of painting that had no predetermined goal, no fixed agenda. In the same way that the participants checked inside themselves, these painters would be doing the same, connecting with the energy of the present, then giving expression to it on the canvas.

Once they started to paint, those who had gathered around them would join in. So, in a way, the experienced painters were acting as guides and this gave them a taste of being in charge.

To find oneself in the position of guiding is an effective way to learn whether you might want to become a facilitator.

Unlived Expression

I knew these painters well, but sometimes they surprised me. For example, one polite and mannerly Englishman, who never imposed himself on others while painting in a group, began with a big move. With one dramatic stroke, he painted a huge dark crescent across the whole canvas.

It was an invitation for the other painters who joined his group to live the quality of bold expression. Some of them, I noticed, were already touched. His action had affected them emotionally and I could guess why.

The way we tend to live our daily lives leaves little room for such honest and bold expression. Most of the time, unfortunately, we find ourselves living in a world of careful calculation and hesitant action. But now, in marked contrast, these participants were being offered an opportunity to live their energy frankly and fearlessly.

In this way, painting serves as a mirror. When you join a group like this, you see both your normal behaviour and your hidden qualities – the inner voices calling you, asking for your help to be released.

Communion: A Healing Experience

Today, working together on these big paintings, people soon became absorbed with the challenge at hand and produced no inter-personal conflicts. Everyone was learning how to dissolve their unique expression, their own way of painting, into an organic union with the others.

This can be an important healing experience, because many of our psychological wounds are created and sustained through separation or alienation – the feeling of becoming an island with no bridge to the rest of humanity.

I've seen it many times, especially in the art world. The assertion of individual ego is generally regarded as a way of feeling good, of claiming the spotlight, making yourself known; but it's also a way of hurting yourself. You can easily become isolated, cut off from the warmth of communion with other people.

Separation dissolves when the claim of the ego – "I am a great artist," "I am the best," or "I will do it my way, no matter what" – is set aside. Then you can use art to heal yourself, because the wound of isolation starts to heal. In this space we create together, we experience the nourishing state of communion and its healing power.

Osho's insight is that the human ego is a false entity, created by each of us in response to our family environment and to the ideas and attitudes given to us by others. Authentic expression of one's true nature happens only when the ego is dissolved. Only then can we sing a song of existence together, like birds singing in the morning sun.

Deeper than Words

Here, healing happens without words and concepts. Why? Because painting is a non-verbal, visual medium. In the human psyche, pictures penetrate deeper than words and touch a more primal space within us. That's why children's books are published with big pictures and few words. Historically, too, self-expression and communication through pictures preceded the invention of complex languages and some ancient cave paintings are thought to have been created more than 40,000 years ago.

I also noticed that people were becoming silent, which to me is a sign that the atmosphere of meditation was slowly having an impact. Personal growth is supported by meditation, which is why I offer Osho's active meditations – mostly Dynamic and Kundalini – as an integral part of my workshops and trainings.

Here's an interesting paradox to chew on: I've just been talking about the healing power of communion that can happen when people cooperate on big paintings. Meditation, on the other hand, gives people the understanding that, essentially, we are each alone.

In fact, both are true. In the group we meet others. In the silent depths of meditation, we meet our inner being in all its purity and stillness. Nobody else can penetrate there. But this is not the loneliness and isolation experienced in the state of ego. It carries with it a deep sense of connection to existence itself.

Resting in Not Knowing

This inner silence has other consequences, too. It teaches us to rest in the space of not knowing, beyond the chatter of thoughts that are constantly trying to tell us what to do. If we listen to our thoughts, then what will emerge on the canvas is just a projection of the mind. But if we can go deeper, touching our silence and innocence, then we look out at the world through fresh eyes; we look at nature and at painting in a totally new and different way.

I was happy with that training. The way people were painting showed their understanding was deepening. I have never been interested in teaching directly; I have never given the participants set-by-step methods and painting techniques.

Rather, I have always provided a situation where they can experience and explore for themselves. Each one has his own way to express. Each one has his own way to be authentic. Each one will move at his own speed.

Exercise: Tunnel of Love

This is a simple, beautiful and very touching exercise in which the whole group experiences what it feels like to give love and to receive love.

Participants choose a partner and then stand opposite each other, side-by-side with other couples, in a long line. So, we end up with two long lines of people facing each other, with just enough room between them to allow one person to walk slowly between the lines.

This is what happens: taking turns and beginning at one end of the tunnel, each participant walks slowly through the tunnel with eyes closed, opening to receiving the love of the whole group. People can softly touch them, caressing the face or hair, whispering words of love.

Once they have gone through the tunnel, they stand at the end and become part of the line again. This exercise is often a strongly emotional experience for people, because it is no small thing to receive so much love and appreciation. One has to open one's heart wide, to be receptive and grateful, and this, as we all know, is not always easy. Those who have been protecting themselves through a tough exterior, or perhaps through pride, may have difficulty opening their hearts to receive. Again, it is an opportunity to see the ego in action and set it aside.

Chapter Thirteen

Self-Portrait: Encountering Yourself

Self-Portrait is one of the most intriguing aspects of my work. It's like operating on yourself, as a surgeon, going deep inside to find your being, to rediscover those qualities that have been buried under your education and social upbringing.

Those qualities have been neglected for many, many years. People don't know the beauty that is hidden inside themselves, so I invite them on a journey to find it through painting a self-portrait.

This part of the training has a different setup. A mirror, large enough in which to see your whole head, is placed at a short distance from the painter, who sits facing it with a board across his knees, or on the floor in front of him. Fixed to the board is a special sheet of paper with a hard, stone-like surface that can be washed without damage.

For Self-Portrait, we use only one colour: a grey gouache. This greyness is an intense, dark colour with just a hint of red and blue, which gives the portraits a dramatic quality. The method here is to apply dark gouache to the paper, then introduce light by wiping some of the paint away with a damp cloth, sponge, or brush. That's how we create the contrast of light and dark that gives shape to the face on the paper.

Drawing What You See

In the beginning, we ignore the paint and start with a pencil. Or, rather, we begin by simply looking at ourselves in the mirror. This, in itself, is a powerful experience.

126

In daily life, we don't normally do this. We look in a mirror to fix our hair, remove a pimple, apply make-up, or trim our beards; we don't just sit and look.

I invite people to look in the mirror, notice what they see about themselves, and then draw what they see on the paper with their pencils. Inevitably, most people begin with the eyes, because eyes are the most expressive part of our body – they are our windows to the personality and to the soul. Next come eyebrows, eyelashes and the nose.

The interesting thing about drawing lines on paper is that they tend to limit and confine the artist. You begin by thinking you're going to create an authentic image of yourself, but pretty soon, after a few pencil strokes, you find yourself stuck in a two-dimensional prison. Most of my participants discover they've drawn a basic cartoon or caricature and then don't know what to do with it.

For many people, this situation is reminiscent of experiences with childhood colouring books. Parents or teachers gave them a picture book with different scenes outlined in thick black lines, and a box of crayons or paints, then told them to colour in the spaces between the lines. In this way, they were taught painting as a rigid division of space, with no options or flexibility.

Undoing Ideas about Portraits

After an hour, when I call everyone together and discuss this issue, they soon get the point: habitually, we are in too much of a hurry to define objects – eyes, nose, chin and so on – but, as a consequence, we don't actually meet ourselves, which is the purpose of this workshop. We remain on the periphery, dealing with the superficial.

At this time, I also point out a common error in portrait painting: the eyes are almost always placed too high on the head, as if the cranium above the eye sockets doesn't exist. In reality, you have as much head above your eyes as you do below. Take a look in the mirror and you'll see.

Such comments can be helpful, because it gives people courage to throw away ready-made concepts and dig into themselves, exploring unknown territory.

Dancing Your Name

One exercise that helps this process is called *Dancing Your Name*. I've already introduced it, earlier in the book, but it's worth mentioning again because it serves the purpose of deepening self-inquiry, which is essential for our project.

I invite everyone to find a partner, then choose who is Partner A and who is Partner B. Partner A begins by announcing his name three times, while at the same time giving expression to his essential being through a dance movement.

For example, someone may say, "Angela, Angela, Angela..." while doing a pirouette. In this way, Partner A dances his name to Partner B, who receives it without comment. Next, they change roles. Partner B dances his, or her, name to Partner A.

During the exercise I ask participants, "When you are received as a dance, how is it for you? When you feel safe to show yourself as you are, what happens to your energy?"

The answer that comes back to me, as I watch these dancing figures, is that slowly they build up their confidence, opening up to each other, realising it is safe to "come out and play," without fear of ridicule. Safety is important when people are taking risks and feeling vulnerable.

Over the years, through leading many groups and trainings, I have come to understand that the best way to create a safe atmosphere is to work with individuals in an open forum, with the rest of the group silently watching.

Individual Sessions: Investigating with Love

Individual sessions are an investigation into personal difficulties, looking to see at which point people have stopped themselves, blocked their feelings, avoided issues, turned away from life. It's not done in an aggressive way. I'm not Sherlock Holmes, looking for clues to expose a wrongdoer. Not at all.

This work is done with love. An individual who asks for one of these sessions knows that my intention is to help; to look together into the darkness of past conditioning and heal the hurt so that we can all benefit in the light of understanding.

The simple fact is: when you hide, you can't work on yourself. You can't flow with your own energy. You can't be in tune with life. Growing up, we learned how to hide our imperfections from others. Gradually, hiding becomes a habit and soon we are hiding from ourselves as well. Once we succeed in hiding from ourselves we are lost, so that's why we need to look again, as adults, to find where we have buried our vitality.

Sharing in this way is contagious. By watching someone who is sharing about his or her difficulties, others start to feel it is really a pity to hide. For what? Why hold on to old habits that do nothing except inhibit our joy?

Exploring Through Touch

The next step in our journey is exploring through touch. Here, I need to mention Helen Keller, the famous American deaf and blind woman who, with the help of her devoted teacher, Anne Sullivan, learned everything about the world through touch. She broke out of her isolation, studied at university, earned a Bachelor of Arts' degree and became an international figure.

I remember one incident in her life. In 1953, she visited India and was introduced to Prime Minister Jawaharlal Nehru. Immediately, she touched his face – that was her way of meeting people. She told him his face "had real nobility and a high-domed brow one needs the gift of a poet to describe...a person that elevates human ideals and goals and shoves the world closer to true civilisation."

This incident inspired me to create self-portraits in a similar way, through touching our own faces. It's not something we normally do unless we need to fix something: rub the eyes, scratch the nose or wipe away some food stains from the mouth.

Touching for touching's sake; touching to say 'hello' to ourselves; these are unusual events. But, for this group, it's an important prelude to painting a self-portrait.

Touch Like a Sculptor

First, I need to make certain preparations, making sure each person has his paper in front of him, a small sponge close at hand and some grey paint in a dish next to it.

"Close your eyes and start touching your face as if you have never touched it in your life," I suggest to the participants.

"Touch with your fingers, with the palms of your hands, with the back of your hands. Touch like a sculptor who is making a head out of clay and water."

As people go deeper into the exercise, I say, "Now, keeping your eyes closed, touch your face with one hand, then with your other hand pick up your sponge, dip it in the grey paint and sculpt the shape that you're feeling onto the paper in front of you."

This is challenging. People are afraid to lose the likeness they've already drawn on the paper, or they're afraid of missing the paper altogether, so some peek out of one eye – it's difficult for them to keep both eyes closed. But with my encouragement they get into the exercise and are soon sponging blindly on the paper.

When I invite them to open their eyes, they are surprised and a little shocked. The portrait drawing has disappeared and there is a grey wash on the paper, with no indication of a head-like shape.

Rather than being disappointed, however, most people feel relieved.

"Finally, I can relax," commented a 45-year-old architect from Sweden. "Somehow, letting go of my image on the paper was like saying goodbye to my identity. It's a relief to realise that I don't need to be 'somebody' anymore."

A Guest of the Mirror

We move on to the next step in our process. It's yet another of my devices for changing the gestalt, changing the normal way we look at the world and at ourselves. If we don't turn everything upside down, we will never get rid of the fixed attitudes in our heads and, as a result, we will never encounter reality directly, without prior opinions.

"Normally, when we look at something, our gaze has an aggressive, penetrating quality," I explain. "Our look is like an arrow, moving toward its target. But this time I want your gaze to be soft and receptive. I want you to be the guest of whomever you see in the mirror. It's as if the person in the mirror is watching you, not the other way around."

When people look into a mirror like this over a period of time, it starts to trigger a lot of issues. Many judgements about ourselves start surfacing. Another very common reaction is that we start seeing our mothers and fathers in the reflection before us.

The first thing that you see is what you are rejecting. For example, if you are saying 'no' to your father, you will see your father, which is one reason why we avoid looking into mirrors in this way. We don't want to be reminded of the parents from whom we are trying to distance ourselves.

My approach, inspired by my love for Family Constellation, is to encourage people to receive the parent in the mirror and welcome what is triggered, even if it is tears, catharsis, angry shouting or deep sobbing.

I teach people how to embrace the parents as a stepping stone to real freedom, with the understanding that pushing them away doesn't work. The very effort to keep parents at a distance strengthens the bonds we are trying to break.

When, for example, the father you are seeing in your portrait is received, then you can begin to understand his perspective. You see the difficulties he faced, you have a glimpse of his emotional life, and you understand that you are an expression of his love and that is why you are here on this Earth. He could have chosen not to have a child, but despite all the challenges, he went through with it.

Remember You Are a Buddha

So, as you can see, my effort in these workshops and trainings is to help people de-automatise their inner world. As we dive deeper into the world of painting, all their assumptions and attitudes are challenged, including basic human relationships.

Why? Because all of these ideas and beliefs make up the central idea of who we think we are and how we view the world.

The fundamental understanding that I carry, which has been transmitted to me by Osho, my spiritual master, is that all of us, in essence, are buddhas. For years, when concluding his evening discourses, he would say to us, "Remember, you are a buddha." Sometimes, making a joke out of it, he'd say things like 'You are all buddhas pretending not to be."

In other words, we are made of the stuff called buddha-consciousness. Our essential nature is that of an awakened being.

Everything else is non-essential; added to us while we grappled with the task of growing up and finding our place in society. We call it our identity, or our personality, and it's within this personality that we find all the blocks and difficulties that prevent us from flowing with life.

Saying 'Yes' to Your Being

A time comes in Self-Portrait when we are able to say 'yes' to our inner being, to the buddha inside. Beyond the imprints of our father and mother, beyond all the crap, we see our original being, looking out at us from the mirror.

That's the point when I say, "Look into your eyes. See how much they shine. Don't waste this opportunity. Receive this energy. Receive yourself through the mirror."

Now the participants begin to understand. This isn't just a class in creating a portrait of themselves. This is a long, deep look inside. This is an encounter with themselves at soul level.

Exercise: Self-Portrait Solo

Painting your self-portrait can be done alone, at home, as well as in a group situation. Set up a painting space where you can relax and not be disturbed. Position the mirror, gather your brushes, sponge, water bucket and your grey gouache mix.

You can work on this self-portrait at any time, but I recommend doing it at night, after dark, using a candle to illuminate your face. The soft candlelight atmosphere lends a sense of mystery to your features and will take you deeper into yourself.

Exercise: Soma Meditation

Sit in front of a mirror, in a comfortable position, so that you can remain motionless for a long time without feeling uncomfortable or being disturbed by others.

Keep your eyes open and look at yourself in the mirror, without moving. Try not to blink. Blinking may happen, but, as far as possible, stare at yourself with unblinking eyes. Breathe normally and stay relaxed.

Several things may occur: you may begin to see many different faces, all of which are somehow reflected in your own face. You may suddenly find that, after a while, your face has simply disappeared from the mirror, leaving you with a sense of 'isness' and nothing else. Or, you may find that your face stays the same, but keeps becoming more profound, taking you deeper and deeper into yourself.

Chapter Fourteen

Self-Portrait: Let There Be Light

Today, the sunlight of India contributes beautifully to the drama of painting a self-portrait. We are occupying our usual place: at one end of a large oval-shaped, marble-floored arena. Formerly, it was an auditorium where Osho gave discourses. Now it has lost its roof and is open to the sky. In the morning, the sunlight filters through the trees surrounding us and gracefully lights up our faces.

I invite the group to study the effect in our mirrors, noting where the light hits the face and how it highlights certain areas, in contrast to those in shadow.

"You can see where the light illuminates your face – it's obvious, no?" I ask the participants. "So, take a sponge, dip it in water, squeeze it, then stroke it across your portrait where you see the light."

This action, as I hinted in the previous chapter, has a remarkable effect. The white surface of the paper emerges from beneath the grey paint, creating light on the face. The novelty of this method of painting surprises and delights everyone. Light does not have to be imposed. It can be revealed.

On a deeper level, I suspect, another understanding may be dawning: darkness is not to be feared, as it has always been, down the ages. Darkness is not the dead-end that it appears to be. With just a stroke or two, it reveals itself as an essential partner in a delightful play of light and dark, like the yin-yang Taoist symbol of ancient times.

Tomatoes, Cauliflowers and Chapatis

To give the painting more depth and realism, participants need to gain a sense of volume and this – in my experience – is best done through imagery, using familiar objects from everyday life.

"So, which kind of face are you?" I inquire. "Are you a tomato or a cauliflower, a cucumber, or an egg?"

It may sound rude, but that's not my intention. Like the famous French painter, Paul Cézanne, I find it greatly helps if I reduce natural forms – such as the human head – to their geometrical essentials.

Sometimes I even ask, "Are you are chapati face?" Chapatis are thin, savoury pancakes which accompany almost every meal in India. They are flat and round. I refer to them because, to be frank, there are many Asian people whose faces, in their basic form, resemble a chapati.

Seeing the head through these familiar images helps to break away from the shallow look that people often create when they first try portrait painting.

Touching with the Eyes

"The portrait you are creating here is not a two-dimensional line drawing," I explain. "When you close your eyes and touch your head with your fingers, this becomes obvious. You can feel it, no? It's a three-dimensional object. Even the back of your head, which you cannot see, can be felt in this way.

"Now, allow your eyes to become extensions of your fingers. Don't touch your head. Rather, look in the mirror. Explore the structure of your face visually, as if you are touching. Where are the cheek bones? Where is the forehead, the eye sockets?"

This connection between seeing and touching is an effective way for people to learn how to perceive texture and depth in a face; how to start 'reading' a face beyond a superficial impression. The morning light supports us. Sunbeams are shafting at an angle through the branches, helping us see the fullness of the head.

Working on Face Muscles

Next, I invite the group to experiment with a Tibetan meditation. It focuses attention on the face. Two partners stand in front of each other, open their mouths wide and start moving their jaw muscles in random fashion, while at the same time holding their hands in front of the chest and wiggling their fingers.

As I've already mentioned, we tend to restrict the movements of the face because we believe this is our 'trademark'. Consciously or unconsciously, we have all spent a great deal of time and effort cultivating a certain 'look' and we want to stick to it.

But if you look at children, their faces are very expressive and constantly in movement. Every emotion, every mood, is naturally written there. They haven't yet learned to cultivate a visual identity for others.

Moving the fingers helps to loosen up the face. The two actions complement each other nicely. There are several therapy techniques employing finger movements because they are closely connected to the brain.

"This is not theatre," I caution, as some participants start to wildly exaggerate their expressions. "You are not performing to entertain somebody else. You are exploring those muscles you ordinarily never move."

Tigers, Elephants and Mice

But it's difficult for people to resist the temptation to play the fool in this exercise, so eventually I relent and go with the energy. This is an opportunity to have fun and at the same time expand our movements beyond the face to include the whole body. As a teacher, I've seen how learning in a playful way can be as effective as with conventional methods, which tend to be rather serious.

Again, simple imagery is the key to the lesson about to be delivered.

"Which animal are you in this moment?" I ask. "Are you a tiger, an elephant, a lion, or a mouse?"

It takes only a moment for everyone to throw themselves into this new exploration. They're already in the mood and soon the whole arena is filled with strange animals, running around...hissing, snarling and squeaking at each other. It's a zoo, a circus and a jungle all rolled into one.

"Make sure your whole body is involved in your movements," I say, above the commotion. "Animals are total beings. Every part of an animal's body moves in harmony, as one organism."

I believe in the body. I trust in the body. I want people to be naturally connected to their bodies because this will give their paintings a sense of authenticity and power. A painting that comes only from the head may win critical praise, but for me it's not a true reflection of a person's individuality.

Saying 'Yes' to Yourself

When the animals get tired of their antics I call them back from the jungle to sit once more before their self-portraits.

138

Slowly, slowly, on this paper in front of us, we are building a temple, a monument to oneself, a house for the soul to be seen in.

"Don't be in a hurry to fix the features," I advise. "Take your time. Focus on basic shapes. Where are the valleys? Where are the hills and promontories? And stay away from the eyes. If you've already put in your eyeballs, take them out again."

Adding eyeballs early in a self-portrait usually turns out to be a disaster. Once you add the eyes, you become paralysed, as if you've written the ending of a novel while only half-way through. The proportion may be wrong, your eyes may be too close together, or too far apart, but you don't want to move.

"What is really important, at every stage of Self-Portrait, is that you are saying 'yes' to yourself, embracing yourself in the mirror," I explain. "This face that you see reflected in the mirror is not you. It is just an entering point on the journey to find your real self, so keep going, keep moving, keep on meeting yourself."

Sleeping Muse

We are still at a stage where it is possible to make significant changes to our portraits, so now I ask everyone, "How wide is your face?"

No talent is required to figure this out. You can measure it with your hands and fingers, then find the same width on the paper. But literal representation must now take a back seat, because I have other ideas.

"Let's make the head really big – as big as you can without going off the sides of the paper," I instruct. Of course, we need to keep the vertical dimension in the same proportion as our new extra-wide head, so this means the rest of the body disappears entirely.

139

"No neck is needed, no shoulders are needed," I say, encouragingly. "Just fill the paper with your head."

At this point, I usually talk about Constantin Brancusi, the Romanian-born sculptor who made his career in France during the early twentieth century. One of Brancusi's most famous works – perhaps the most famous – is called *Sleeping Muse*.

Brancusi was really a revolutionary, because all he carved was a head – and a very thin head at that. The head is lying down, on its side, as if on a pillow, and the features are indicated, or suggested, with minimal effort. The eyes, nose and mouth are almost non-existential and, yet, you can tell everything about the beauty of sleep, the peace and relaxation of rest. It's a complete statement.

My point is: communicating a state of being doesn't need literal representation. It doesn't need much attention to detail. It can be done in other ways...through basic form, for example.

It Shows in the Painting

Slowly, the group participants are absorbing my unconventional way of creating self-portraits and the effect starts to show in their creations.

Some people are still busy with: "How do I look? Do I look good, or not? Am I going to make it, or not?" And their fear reflects on the paper.

An experienced teacher doesn't need to talk and ask questions. I can look at a portrait and know exactly what people are thinking, where people are in their process, what fears are being encountered, in which way their meditation is growing ☐ everything.

People are shocked when I say things to them, like "All your life you have been afraid of darkness."

"That's true, but how do you know that about me?" they ask, in surprise.

I just point to the painting and say, "It shows."

Modelling for Others

Before we bring Self-Portrait to its conclusion, I guide the group into several sessions of painting each other's portraits. This process offers two important experiences: painting and modelling. Of the two, the experience of being a model is more rewarding, especially at this stage of our workshop.

One of the strongest understandings in my life came when I was a model for a sculptor. I was sitting for five hours a day while he shaped my face in clay. I was an art student, 20 years old, knowing nothing about meditation.

The sculptor was a master of his art. Each time he completed a sculpture of my face, I could see a different quality in it, as if the face was just a vehicle for deeper forces to emerge and find expression. The real thing was not the face, not the physical form, but the beauty of the being within the form.

Gradually, in this way, I began to realise that life exists independently of the body. It is an inner light shining out of the eyes, through the skin, radiating from some unknown source.

I want my students to have this experience: becoming aware of their inner qualities by being a model. The portraits don't have to be masterful. Even if they are painted in a chaotic, Picasso-like way, full of abstraction and distortion, something of the model's essence will still be seen.

One more thing: by exposing yourself to another person, while he or she is painting you, looking deeply into you, you can also look more deeply into yourself.

You can use the penetrating gaze of your partner to become more conscious of your own being. When this happens, your natural inner beauty starts to shine through. This is the magic of self-awareness.

Every 15 minutes, I ring the bell, inviting the partners to change roles, switching between modelling and painting. Then, when the session is over, they look together at the portraits and share their experiences.

Completing the Picture

Painting portraits with a partner has brought us to the final stage of our workshop, because in these quick portraits they have been painting the eyes. So now we can add this final touch to the self-portraits as well.

"Look into your eyeballs; how big are they?" I ask the group. "Relax your eyes, look into the mirror and check their size, not only with a measuring stick – anyone can do that – but using your inner feeling, trusting your connection with the face in the mirror.

"Let go of any ideas about you and your inner beauty. You have to see beyond the physical, behind the facade. What is there, behind the mask?"

With my encouragement, they start seeing more depth in their own reflections and some succeed in making really beautiful eyes, sparkling with hidden qualities.

Here, at the very end of the process, I also have to intervene and catch the moment when a self-portrait is complete. The painters have been slowly building up their creations over three days and now they must be careful not to spoil them by going on too long.

"Stop, right there!" I advise one participant. "When beauty reveals itself like a gift, don't interfere. Greed kills everything.

Getting in touch with your being doesn't mean you have to be perfect; adding each little detail of the nose, mouth, this and that...

"No, when you touch some mystery and it is reflected on your paper, don't go on. You have captured the spirit. Now leave it alone."

Two Characters: Innocence and Passion

In the end, I pick two paintings for comment. One is by a shy Taiwanese woman called Shunyo; the other, by an Englishman called Peter.

Shunyo is innocent and hesitant, with a tendency toward self-doubt and fear of criticism, but essentially a very truthful person.

Throughout this workshop, she has been behaving as if she knows nothing about painting. Naturally, you get the impression, since this person knows nothing, she won't be capable of producing anything remarkable.

But her self-portrait is so beautiful that, looking at it, you almost stop breathing!

"Attitude makes a portrait," I tell the group, holding it up for everyone to see. "Shunyo is no expert. She is a beginner, really. It shows what can happen when you just follow the method I outlined for you. She never used a paintbrush, just a sponge, but you can clearly see the being in the painting."

Peter is a total contrast: fiery, assertive, self-confident. Shortly before the workshop he was behaving like an angry man, arguing with the Resort's administration, fighting with the managers. He was super-happy during the group, but with the same gusto and passion.

"His portrait reflects his passion – you can't miss it!" I comment.

Innocence and passion...two different qualities and two remarkable self-portraits. And they are not alone. Almost all the paintings, however sophisticated or naive, carry a taste of the inner being that looked into the mirror, saw itself reflected, and manifested itself on the paper. That's the beauty of self-portrait painting.

Combining Self-Portrait with Family Constellation

Here is an exercise that you can do at home while painting a self-portrait, to deepen your sense of who is being painted.

Covering your left eye with an eye-patch, or scarf, look into the mirror, seeing yourself only through your right eye.

As we already know, the right eye represents the male energy in us, and here, particularly, we are inviting the energy of the father to manifest in front of us.

You are meeting your father, his essence, his qualities. Ask yourself, "Can I say 'yes' to these qualities and give them expression in my self-portrait?"

When you have done this for a few minutes, switch over and cover your right eye with the eye-patch, looking into the mirror only with your left eye. Here, you are invoking the qualities of your mother. Can you receive them, as well?

After a few minutes, remove the eye-patch and look into the mirror with both eyes with a feeling of gratitude in your heart, accepting the qualities of both your parents.

This is the moment to let your eyes shine with the radiance of your inner light. Simply say 'yes' to this shine and it will transform your painting.

Your Disappearing Face

For this exercise, make a self-portrait, representing what you see in the mirror. Then, at a certain point, when all your features are present, cover the whole face with gouache until it is completely covered and blank.

How is it for you to see your face disappear in this way? For many people it is a shock, but also a relaxation. The tension of clinging to a certain appearance and identity has gone.

Now, you can bring your face back in a totally new way. Take your sponge and wipe away some of the gouache, allowing the white of the paper to appear from behind the grey wash.

Slowly, you can paint your face using only a sponge to create its shape and features. It is a beautiful experience to see your face appearing out of darkness in this way.

Chapter Fifteen

Balancing Opposites

The issue of balancing opposites faces anybody who wishes to learn art therapy. In life, one has to learn from every angle, but we have been conditioned to choose one over the other. To give an obvious example, light has been given a good reputation, whereas darkness has been associated with evil and 'dark deeds'.

In a way, it's understandable, because in the old days, before electric light, darkness could be a threat – the cover for a sudden attack by an unseen enemy, or by a wild animal. But it's become a widespread and unfortunate social paradigm, rooted in religious dualities such as good and evil, heaven and hell, God and Devil.

This has become an inbuilt psychology in us all. That's the reason why it is difficult for us to say 'yes' to opposites. Yet we need to overcome this obstacle and bring opposing polarities into our paintings without hesitation.

You may not have thought about it in this way, but opposites are the very nature of nature itself. Winter and summer, day and night, good times and bad times...this is how the natural universe functions.

Human beings, however, have been endowed with the privilege – whether it's a blessing or a curse, I can't really say – of being able to interfere with this natural balance. They can choose, and the more I work with people, the more I see their tendency to choose one polarity and reject the other.

Their choices are reflected in their paintings. For example, if they are saying 'no' to their negativity, then most probably their paintings are going to have a light feeling. Lots of light colours but no black, no darkness. This psychological tendency to choose good over bad, positive over negative, doesn't allow their inner darkness to find outer expression.

Three-Dimensional Painting

Painting is a two-dimensional phenomenon: horizontal and vertical movements on a flat piece of paper. On this surface, the artist needs to deceive the eye and create a sense of three-dimensional reality.

There is a particular style, practised since Roman times, called *trompe l'œil*, which takes three-dimensional painting to the extreme, creating optical illusions, such as water flowing uphill, people walking upside down and all kinds of bizarre paradoxes.

To a lesser degree, all painters need to be aware of this important aspect of art. To make a painting three-dimensional, you need to understand that if you don't allow darkness there will be no contrast to light. Hence, there will be no sense of depth. Opposites create contrast. Contrast creates depth.

With me, participants don't learn three-dimensional techniques directly. Instead, they are invited to focus on their own psychology: what they are expressing, what they are hiding and suppressing. If they have a problem, or an issue that needs addressing – such as a shallow approach and a tendency towards flatness – then sooner or later it will reflect on the paper in front of them and we will deal with it as a reflection of their inner world. There is no need for a lot of technical input.

Also, I invite them to notice what opinions they have of each other's work, because it's inevitable that when you criticise another person's work you are making a projection and denying something in yourself.

Criticising Paintings

As I've said before, criticism inhibits creativity, judgements limit our vision, so I've developed ways to bypass it. One method is to hang all our paintings on the walls around the room, then invite the participants to check them out and stand in front of a painting they don't like, or which they think is ugly.

It can be any painting except their own. I encourage them to say out loud statements, like "I wouldn't want to paint like that" and then start talking to the painting as if talking to a person, putting out all their judgements:

"You are too dark...too much of a mess...too confusing..." etc.

After a while, I ask people to use a finger to point to the area of the painting they think is the ugliest. "Is it the whole painting, or just a small part of it that you are judging?" I ask them. To emphasise the situation, I ask them to adopt a certain body posture which reflects how they are feeling about the ugly spot, then close their eyes and feel it inside.

Then, after some moments, I ask people to open their eyes, relax the body and be receptive, in a positive way, to whatever they find ugly in the painting, welcoming it into their hearts.

"Unless we can welcome and accept those things we consider to be ugly as well as the things we find beautiful, then depth in one's painting is not possible," I explain.

Dancers and Sculptors

Another, similar approach, is to display all our paintings, invite people to stand in front of one they dislike, and then we put on music.

"If this painting makes you dance, what kind of dance will it be?" I ask people. "Receive this painting in a soft way and let your body respond to what your heart is feeling."

Some people feel an earthy quality, so their bodies make slow movements that reach down towards the ground. Others feel light and airy, so they are almost on tiptoe, reaching upwards as they move to the music.

"If you translate this painting into sculpture what kind of posture will it have?" I inquire.

In response, they adopt all sorts of poses and I see glimpses of Rodin's *Thinker*, Michelangelo's *Moses,* and India's dancing *Nataraj* statue of Shiva.

"Stop! No more movement! Now, in this unmoving, frozen state, look at the painting. Using your eyes as a neutral window, receive the painting into the sculpture you are making with your body, so the sculpture is meeting the painting, and the painting is meeting the sculpture."

In this way, participants are able to embody, absorb, accept and appreciate those qualities in the painting that they were initially rejecting.

Sculpting Each Other

This is an exercise for two partners, in which one is a sculptor and the other is the sculpture. Here, we do not focus on criticism, but on bringing out essential qualities in each other. Moving between the polarities of criticism and appreciation is an effective way of integrating all our opinions, good and bad.

The sculptor is invited to sculpt his partner's essence and beauty by fixing her posture according his own feelings.

The one who is being sculpted simply adopts whatever posture or position the sculptor makes, using the arms, legs, head and torso.

After some time, the sculptor can stand back and observe his work from different angles. When the work is complete, all the sculpted people remain frozen while the sculptors walk around the room, looking at each other's work, seeing the beauty of all these different human forms.

The point of this exercise is to experience how we can intuitively get a sense of the essential qualities of each person, bringing them out into the light of day and giving them shape and form.

Transparent Sharing

Next, we borrow a technique from the Zen-style method of inquiry known in Osho Therapy as "Who is In?"

In this exercise, two people sit facing each other. One speaks for five minutes while the other simply listens, without comment. Then a bell rings and they reverse roles. There is no dialogue, no conversation. One speaks while the other remains a witness – present, alert, silently listening.

In my version of this method, one partner puts out his criticism and judgement of the painting while the other listens without comment.

It can be a magical experience. The silent partner is not giving any advice, but a new clarity soon arises in the one who is speaking as his judgements are verbalised and dissolved.

Exploring Darkness

In daily life, we all go through difficult times and these can easily create stress and make us tense. However, a lot of this stress is unnecessary. If we can relax and accept the situation, most problems resolve themselves in their own time.

But that's just the problem – we can't wait. Rather, we get panicky. We want to change things fast. When darkness comes, we want to get out of it and move towards the light. Therefore, an important task in helping people to balance opposites is to make them comfortable with darkness.

In Pune, I take them down into the Resort's underground therapy chambers where it is possible to create an atmosphere of total darkness. For most people, this is a very unusual experience. Rarely, if ever, do we choose to put ourselves in a total blackout.

I've written about this extensively in my previous book, *ReAwakening of Art*, but it's worth going over again because it's an essential process in personal transformation.

A Symbolic Struggle

Each participant stands close to the room's padded walls and the lights are turned off. I invite them to face the wall and to remember moments in their lives when they were overtaken by 'dark' feelings of hopelessness, fear of failure, situations where they felt trapped and so on.

Symbolically, I invite them to push against this darkness by pushing hard against the wall while remembering these impossible situations from their lives.

It's symbolic, but effective. In this atmosphere of total darkness, it's easy for people to connect with an overwhelming feeling of hopelessness. The struggle to achieve what we think will make us happy and the fight to get rid of what we think makes us unhappy; this inner conflict has been going on a long time in everyone's life.

There is another level, too. Darkness is associated with death. This all-pervading space of blackness, of nothingness, has a feeling of finality. It looks like the end of everything.

Have you noticed how, at the end of almost every movie, the credits roll up the screen against a black background? Have you noticed how almost all movies, all dramas, end by fading into black?

It's not without significance. Darkness is the end of our story. Darkness is death. There seems to be no way out, with no bottom to it, no further step to take in any direction. In terms of colour, too, we have reached the end – darker than black doesn't exist.

Change the Gestalt: Relaxing into Darkness

I encourage people to continue pushing against the walls for at least 15 minutes and then create the opportunity for a dramatic change in gestalt.

"Now stop pushing and become silent," I tell them. "Turn around slowly and lean back against the wall. Instead of treating it as your enemy, see if you can feel supported by the darkness that surrounds you."

As they stop struggling and relax into the arms of darkness, I continue, "Darkness is the absence of light. In a way, it goes deeper than light, because light comes and goes; light has a transient quality. Even our sun will burn out one day, grow dim and then go dark.

"Darkness is an eternal quality of existence, a universal principle, neither negative nor positive. And it is always there. From this darkness we come. To this darkness we return."

I don't encourage emotional expression at this point, because the connection to darkness goes deeper in silence, but sometimes it happens on its own.

After this experience has settled in us all, I turn on the lights and guide people into painting, using only black. Setting out paper and ink in the underground chamber, I invite participants to express through painting what happened to them during the first two phases of the darkness exercise. Then, after a few minutes when they are fully absorbed in their painting, I suddenly turn off the lights.

"Keep your eyes open and continue to use your brush on the paper," I tell them.

There is something magical about painting blindly – really blindly. I can guarantee that nobody in this group has done such a thing before. It is a unique sensation: you are painting, but you can't see *what* you are painting. Your eyes are open, your hand is moving, painting is happening...yet all you can see is darkness, darkness, darkness.

In such a situation, you are helpless and also innocent, because none of your normal control mechanisms can function. Your sense of the painting that you wish to create is now coming from inside you – it belongs to your interior rather than mental ideas.

When sight is impossible, other senses now become more alive – especially touch. For example, I guide people to dip their fingers in water and touch the paper with their hands, forgetting for a moment that they are painting, just focusing on the sense of touch.

Next, I switch on the light and invite people to cover their paintings entirely in black ink, telling them, "With each stroke of black that you make on the paper, you are becoming more and more a friend with darkness."

When the transition is complete and the whole paper is black, I again turn off the lights and invite people to stare into darkness, in a relaxed and receptive way, without blinking the eyes, for several minutes:

"Let darkness fill your being. You are receiving darkness through your eyes; you are breathing darkness."

Balancing Black and White

After a while, I light a small candle.

"One small candle light can dispel the entire darkness from this room," I explain. "Now let us gaze softly at the candle light in the same relaxed way, without blinking our eyes, for a few minutes."

After a while, I give out pots of white paint, because the next step is also significant. First, we moved away from light into darkness. Now we are moving back from darkness to light.

Because people's papers are entirely covered with black ink, I invite them to take a clean brush, dip it in the white paint, hold it above the paper and let the colour drip onto the blackness. The first drip of white on the dark black painting is powerful and contains a message: even a small amount of light can dispel darkness.

Once you understand this point, your relationship to your psychological problems takes a new turn.

I do it this way because, when simply dripping from above, you can't control how you want to paint, so there is no alternative but to be playful about it, enjoying a sense of freshness and wonder.

Gradually, the white colour spreads out, covering the black…in places melting and merging with it.

In this way, we play with black and white, gaining flexibility to move in both directions: from darkness to light, from light to darkness. Gradually, we are moving into a state of balance, in which opposites are allowed and embraced. If there is too much darkness, light can be brought in. If there is too much light, more darkness can be added. There are no dead ends, no full stops on this journey.

In our normal, day-to-day life, we tend to avoid facing darkness because it reminds us of death, of fear, of dark moments in our life. But through this kind of session, one can experience that darkness is our home, our foundation.

Once this understanding settles and balance is restored between light and darkness, it also affects our psychological outlook on life, creating the possibility for more harmony. That's really all one has to learn in life.

Chapter Sixteen

Nature Painting

If you really look at nature, you see that only contrast exists. Look down into the roots of a cherry tree and the earth seems so dark, but when you raise your eyes to the branches above your head, you see an explosion of pink and white blossoms.

There is a deep connection between the inner and outer nature of human beings, and the inner and outer nature of nature itself. The more we understand our own interiority, the more we see the magical harmony and beauty of the natural world around us. And part of that understanding comes with embracing and balancing opposites.

An obvious example is *The Starry Night*, one of Vincent van Gogh's most famous paintings and perhaps his greatest achievement. Created in 1889, it depicts the night-time view out of his sanatorium window at Saint-Rémy-de-Provence in southern France.

Huge stars swirl brightly against a dark blue sky, above an even darker landscape. But the most powerful element in the picture, which contrasts dramatically with the stars and highlights their brilliance, is the huge black shape of a cypress tree dominating the foreground. That's the stroke of genius that shows van Gogh's courage and passion.

Another interesting aspect, which van Gogh explained in a letter to his brother Theo, is that while painting The Starry Night he cast aside concern about 'trompe l'œil precision' in favour of strong colours and the power of imagery.

In other words, you don't have to be too worried about three-dimensional precision when trying to create a sense of depth. Colour alone can do it.

Psychological Approach

I want my participants to understand the need for three-dimensional perspectives, and also the power of contrasting light and dark paints, but, as I hinted earlier, I rely mainly on deepening their psychological understanding.

I don't need to teach many painting techniques to people. I know that if they are motivated to explore their interiority, becoming aware of how they are suppressing energy, emotions and fears, they will naturally begin to include darkness in their paintings, balancing it with light. Then healing happens naturally.

For example, on one occasion, as we ended this exercise, a young Swiss woman started crying. When I asked her what was happening, she replied, "I've never used black in my life. I've been studying art for 12 years and never used black because, somehow, it's too intense. Now I see how much I've been avoiding this colour, because it reminds me of death."

One more anecdote may help to illustrate the point. At the end of a series of workshops in Pune, we hang all our paintings in an exhibition around the big open space known as Buddha Grove. Many of the paintings have been done in nature and when all these paintings are hanging together they create a vivid explosion of trees and leaves and tangled undergrowth.

But in the strong Indian sun the brilliant colours soon start to fade, so after a few days I suggested that – if the participants felt like it – they could use inks to brighten up their paintings.

Inks are transparent. They don't usually interfere with the basic structure of a painting, but they can bring new vibrancy into the colours. And, just through the act of throwing the ink on your painting, you are immediately connecting with life energy – you start sensing that life is literally 'in my hands'.

Adding inks to an existing painting can be a helpful and transforming part of art therapy. You are not saying 'no' to the past, but rather seeing 'through' the painting after a new layer has been added. That's basically what I want to teach: the new is not the negation of the past, but by receiving and honouring the past a different 'newness' will arise.

Then I saw a shy Japanese woman, who had confessed during the workshops that she was very traditional in her outlook on life – conforming to the rules of society, the parents, the husband – suddenly throw black ink right across the top of her painting, creating a new, dramatically dark form, almost like van Gogh's black tree.

She didn't care that the use of inks at this late stage was supposed to be only a touching-up exercise. She didn't care that her painting was supposed to be already finished. She felt free to go with the energy of the moment.

"I feel much freer to express myself now," she explained, with a rebellious smile on her face. "Nature painting has had a big influence on my primal painting and I feel ready to explore and expand."

What Do We Learn from Nature Painting?

Painting the nature that surrounds us, we learn how to be natural and simple, just like the plants, trees and flowers.

They are making no effort to be beautiful, but just through being themselves – not trying to be anything else – they radiate their natural beauty.

Nobody is teaching a lotus flower how to be a better lotus flower. Nobody is teaching a pine tree how to grow taller and be better than the other trees. They don't interfere with each other and yet they all somehow find room to express themselves in their natural splendour.

It is a big lesson for us humans, who seem to spend a great deal of time, money and effort trying to impress others by distorting our natural qualities.

This is how Osho Art Therapists learn from nature. You are just a friend who shares his, or her, creativity with others out of a spontaneous overflow of energy. Some of you will be sensitive and strong, like ancient trees who have gone through many different seasons. Some will be delicate and wild, like pretty meadow flowers reaching for the morning sun.

We all have the potential to experience a deep rapport with nature. Osho tells a story from his own childhood that illustrates this point: he used to enjoy sitting under a certain tree in his village and one day, just before he was leaving for university, he felt the tree was weeping. The tree understood that this was the time to say goodbye. And when Osho returned, many months later, he found the tree had gone. It had been cut down as part of a street improvement scheme.

Nature's Abundance

My work is to help people remember that nature is abundantly rich, endlessly beautiful and continuously in flux...day turning into night, winter turning into summer, climates shifting, plants growing, flowers blossoming...and it's not just a mental understanding.

159

On a deeper level, I want participants to feel, inside themselves, their own connection with nature. Through painting, they experience that they are part of it.

Nature is offering us a spectacle of infinite variety, but most of it remains beyond our perception because we have too many fixed concepts. We have labelled everything: "This is a tree, that is a rose...this is alive, that is dead...this is beautiful, that is ugly."

Labels like these work like a screen in front of our eyes. Labelling things makes them static and fixed.

The most common objects are the most difficult to free from the grasp of our concepts, because we're sure we already know them. When we sit down in front of a grove of bamboos to paint it, do we see these bamboos fresh and vibrant, dancing in the breeze, or do we see an idea that's already been formed in our heads? We know bamboos are hollow, with rings on their stems, yellowish in colour and with green spiky-looking leaves. Will we apply these ideas to the canvas, or will we paint the living bamboos in front of us?

How do we return to the space of child-like wonder, without prejudice, when each moment was new – as if looking at the world for the very first time? If people can learn this, then most of their problems are already gone. One learns to drop the past and willingly respond to each situation afresh.

Taking Nature 'Photos'

This exercise is done in pairs. One partner closes his eyes and is led by the hand into natural surroundings where there is an abundance of nature.

The partner who is the guide leads the 'blind' partner close to a flower, or branch, or some aspect of nature that attracts his attention.

160

Then he squeezes the hand of the 'blind' partner who, for one instant, opens his eyes and then immediately closes them again.

It is just like taking a photo, or snapshot, with a camera. It has an interesting effect on the mind. In that split second there is no time for the mind to figure out what is being seen, and yet the brain receives a vivid image of colour and pattern. You can't apply your knowledge about nature; there is no time. You simply get an impression of shapes and colours as an abstraction. In this way you can capture the real beauty of nature.

Dancing the Tree

Another way to develop rapport with nature is to explore 'Dancing a Tree'. It may sound odd, but if you try it, you will find it soon makes you intimate with nature, giving you the opportunity to become one with it. The exercise is simple: stand in front, or near, a tree of your choice. Let's say, for example, you choose a bamboo. Tune into the bamboo and begin your dance, echoing its shape, reflecting its quality, mirroring its bending branches and its falling leaves. Lose yourself in the dance and become the bamboo.

When you sit down to paint the tree, your whole feeling about it will have been transformed.

Lessons from Calligraphy

Calligraphy helps with nature painting in many ways. It is essentially a spontaneous movement of energy in which your hand that is holding the brush – filled with black ink – dances across a blank white sheet of paper.

Try doing the same thing with your paint brushes when painting nature. Let your hand that is holding the brush dance across the paper, reflecting the nature you see before you. In a way, you are not doing it. Nature is painting itself through you.

Remember that calligraphy demands a high level of body awareness: your body posture needs to be relaxed, your hands and shoulders free of tension. Then empty yourself in a moment of meditation and spontaneously move into action: once you start the movement there should be no hesitation, no going back. Be like a compass: your centre is unmoving and only the end of the needle is seeking and searching the right direction. It is action through inaction.

Exploring Male and Female

Nature painting offers us an opportunity to explore and express our understanding of the male and female polarities within us.

Closing the left eye, we look at nature only through the right eye, which gives us access to the male principle within us. Ask yourself: How does this 'inner man' look at nature? How does he connect with the plants and trees surrounding him? What catches his interest? What kind of brush does he choose and which colour does he dip it in? How does he make his strokes on the paper?

Then, after a few minutes, allow the female energy to emerge. Close your right eye and look at nature through your left eye, giving a free hand to your 'inner woman' to come out and express herself. You can switch between the two energies, offering them both the chance to be creative, and perhaps creating a harmonious flow between them, as they take turns to commune with nature.

Chapter Seventeen

Form and No Form

We are accustomed to form. We are educated to expect it and we tend to become anxious when it's missing, especially in our approach to painting. When we were small children, our busy parents were looking for ways to keep us occupied, so they bought us colouring books and crayons. With the best of intentions, they showed us all the pretty pictures in the book, nicely drawn with black lines – ships, houses, dolls, flowers, happy-looking people – and told us how to use the crayons to colour in the blank spaces inside the lines.

So, in almost every country, children grow up with the idea that painting is a process of creating forms with lines, then filling in the blank spaces with colour. The memory of those early experiences goes deep and so governs our attitudes. It doesn't occur to us that a line is just our invention, with little or no existence in the natural world.

We see lines everywhere. To give just one example: as therapists, we tend to draw a line between ourselves and our clients. It reflects the importance we give to division and categorisation as ways to control and comprehend our world.

The Osho approach to therapy is rather different. You don't look at the client as a problem to be fixed, but rather as a friend with whom you can share your understanding.

Lines Are an Illusion

If you look at nature, whatever you see is not a line. Even the finest line is not really a line. The object you're looking at always has volume, mass, roundness, a graspable form.

Lines are an illusion. You look at a tree, silhouetted against a light sky, and it seems as if it has lines around every branch, created by the contrast of dark against light. But when you walk over to the tree, all the lines change or disappear.

Just put your arms around the tree and hug it. Where are the lines? Where have they gone? Then you realise: your perception of the tree is a changing, mutating flux, depending on distance, contrast, the time of day, the wind in the branches...all the variables of its motion and the surrounding environment.

A Loosening Up Process

My challenge is to help people overcome the fixed ideas inside their heads and move from form to no-form in their approach to painting. It is quite a task, because we have to start afresh. Even though great seers like Gautam Buddha have reminded us, from time to time, that form and no-form are interchangeable and, deep down, one and the same phenomenon, we have a strong, conventional impulse to cling to form.

Many of the exercises already described in this book are helpful as a loosening up process: tearing up paper, criticising paintings, partner painting and painting in the dark; there are lots of different ways to dissolve our rigid ways of looking at life.

Slowly, participants begin to understand the two-dimensional trick that has been played on them by thinking in old, conventional ways, and instead can begin to embrace the fluidity and mystery of the natural world surrounding them.

The next question, naturally enough, is how to translate this new understanding onto a flat canvas in front of them? All painters in the past – geniuses and amateurs alike – have struggled with this task.

From Tangible to Intangible

For example, it's easy to paint the features of a human face because it's a matter of observation. Once you start looking at the face as it really is, with all the nuances and dimensions revealed in the section about the Self-Portrait, this becomes relatively easy.

The challenge is to bring across the character within the face, the inner 'happening' beneath the outer form, which has an intangible quality. You can see it, but you can't touch it – not with your fingers, anyway. Our task, therefore, is to make the intangible tangible.

The word 'tangible' is interesting. It's defined as "capable of being touched" or "discernible by touch." Yet we rarely use this word in relation to our hands or fingers. More often than not, it's used to convey an impression gathered from all our senses and our intuition.

For example, one might say, "There was a tangible atmosphere of excitement in the room as the guests waited for the prince and princess to appear."

This kind of 'tangible' feeling is important in my workshops. It includes touch, but goes wider and deeper, embracing feelings, smell and intuitive connection. It's a bit like a small baby feeding at her mother's breast – a total sensory experience. All of us carry an organic sense of 'touch' from those early breastfeeding days.

Again, many of the exercises already described can help with this process, especially abandoning the old style of painting while standing in front of an easel. When you get down on the floor, when you use sponges and your own hands to paint, as well as brushes, this 'tangible' quality soon comes back.

This, in turn, makes it easier to connect with the intangible. You're already on the same wavelength as the inner qualities you want to express.

Fixed Ideas are Limiting

Our inner landscape is endlessly rich. However, when we sit down in front of a blank piece of paper we usually try to give expression to a fixed idea that already exists in our heads, which tends to be limiting.

That's why, when painters are rewarded with public recognition and commercial success, they usually stick to a certain style. At the most, they will include a little innovation from time to time, cautiously refining their style, but basically nothing changes.

Here, I would like to mention my mother who was a haiku poet. She gave her life; not only to the art of being a mother and wife, but also to being a poet who sings a song of nature. It was from her that I learned to live as a part of nature and sing from my heart with simplicity, love and respect.

Such a person is innocent, loving and careful not to intrude into other people's lives. Two months before she died, I came back to Japan to take care of her. Each day, when the time of leaving was coming closer, she usually would say to me, "Stay with me a little longer." But one day, when I was leaving, she didn't say anything, so I asked, "Is it okay that I leave you alone?"

She sometimes needed assistance because of her back problem, but she said to me, "Yes, you can go. People are waiting for you and I can take care of myself. Be kind to people."

That was her last message to me. I answered her, "Well, if I feel like being kind, I do so. But if I don't feel like it, I don't." She simply looked at me, so sad, and didn't say anything.

My mother's comment had a big impact on me and it got me thinking: What is the real meaning of kindness and help? It's a question that is often with me when I work with people.

The attitude of the therapist is important. Kindness is a quality that is universally admired, but it will prove to be of help only if it is free of unconscious patterns. Kindness, in its purest form, is an open-hearted sharing that inspires and encourages others, but does not in any way make them feel obligated or in debt to you.

True kindness and freedom walk hand-in-hand.

Abstract Painting: Forms and No Forms

If you can manage *not* to apply your ideas to the act of painting, you become aware of the open invitation offered by the natural world to expand your vision: colour combinations are overlapping, darkness is contrasting with light and stillness is transforming into movement. Some kind of newness is presenting itself at every moment.

The beauty of abstract painting is that it helps us melt the rigid forms inside our minds and embrace this newness that's surrounding us. And this is one way to introduce people to the experience of no form: to abandon ideas about painting 'something' – some object, some portrait – and move into abstraction.

However, I have to say, it's not easy. Once my participants get past the initial, spontaneous burst of excitement in splashing colours randomly on the paper, many of them run into difficulty. Over the years, I've been watching people struggle with this task, and I've noticed that women, especially, find it difficult to allow a painting to be abstract.

It seems that female psychology associates more strongly with finite objects: flowers, homes, bedding, clothes, etc. Men find abstraction easier; maybe they are more philosophically inclined, thinking about vague concepts like God, universal principles, the theory of relativity □ something far away and less concrete □ so they can more easily shift into the vagueness of abstract painting.

The world of no-form is also the world of no-mind, which is the Zen approach to spirituality and meditation. In Zen, meditation takes you beyond the form into the formless, beyond words into silence, beyond matter into emptiness.

Sometimes I guide people to paint on the same paper, again and again, without creating form or reaching completion and this can be a challenging task. How does one move ahead, into the new? Everybody wants to create something unique and new, but the new is possible only if we say 'yes' to ourselves as we are. If we can do this, each moment, then we have an authentic place from which to move forward. Then one gains a sense of harmony, which we experience as falling in tune with life. This, in turn, is nothing but an ongoing flow of creativity.

What has already been painted, is now the past. And, as we have seen in Family Constellation, when we look at the past with love and respect, we become free of it. Love and acceptance of what has already happened makes us free.

Abstraction in painting is a kind of freedom, but the expression of this freedom should not come from concepts and ideas. It should be intuitive, spontaneous and adventurous.

A Psychological Approach

Form is introduced through the mind. Even abstract painting relies on form, but it is less fixed. What was the attraction of Jackson Pollock's paintings? He became a major figure in the abstract expressionist movement, using a drip technique that created flexible, surrealistic forms.

As I mentioned in my first book, *ReAwakening of Art*, Jackson Pollock was inspired by calligraphy, but he didn't understand that this kind of abstract expressionism goes hand-in-hand with meditation. Having bid farewell to form, he became lost in his own formlessness and arrived at a dead end. For him, death was the only exit.

So, when I say I'm teaching the art of no-form painting, I mean it in a meditative way. As soon as a paintbrush touches the paper, shape and form are created, but my participants learn not to become attached to them. They learn to move, to change, to 'go with the flow', allowing their paintings to take any direction without holding onto any of the forms they are creating.

It is a joyous experience to focus one's attention in the present moment, watching the changes that occur on the paper. This was Pollock's contribution: he was capable of bringing art into the present moment, breaking out of the conceptual ideas of his time. But it is not easy, because of our educational background, because of our old idea that a painting "has to look like something."

To paint accidentally, with all forms and colours dissolving into each other is challenging. If you keep allowing the painting to change in this way, it becomes deeper and deeper. One form overlays another form and this combination gives rise to a third shape, which then merges with a fourth shape on some other part of the painting.

Usually, I let the participants paint again and again on the same paper, sometimes exchanging with a partner to break out of their own patterns and tendencies.

As a painting develops, shapes are bound to arise which remind one of certain forms, which in turn are likely to create stories. For example, if a round shape begins to look like an apple, then you can easily imagine Adam and Eve in the Garden of Eden and, once they are brought on, behind them comes the whole Bible.

My work is to keep people rooted in the 'isness' of a painting without creating stories and interpretations. Once you start painting in this way, you experience an ongoing journey of creativity, discovering unknown forms that somehow just appear on the paper in front of you. They are not the forms that you had decided in your head. They are a surprise.

I would like to mention Osho's paintings here. He painted on the blank pages at the beginning of the books he read and loved. He collected a whole library over the years. There are hundreds of these paintings and they are all abstractions.

Osho didn't go to art school, but his way of painting is fresh and takes us into a new world. Looking at them we start sensing lightness and clarity, with mysterious and transparent overlaps of colour and form. The forms are not painted from the mind, but born out of the present moment.

This reminds me of an insight I had when painting an illustration of the full moon for a book of Osho's discourses on Zen. I suddenly understood that perfection is not outside me. If I am centred, I am already perfect and whatever artistic expression comes out of this space is going to create a perfect full moon on the paper.

One day, Osho surprised me by inviting me to take a look in his dining room. Entering the room, I was thrilled by a multi-layered vision. I saw a huge glass window, tinted blue, that looked out onto the jungle-like foliage of Osho's garden. This is where he sat, every day, while taking his meals. A large black and white photo of Osho, hanging in another part of the dining room, was reflected in the glass window. At the same time, looking through the glass, I could see the inter-woven mass of greenery – plants, bushes and trees, all overlapping. And further back, behind it all, a huge blue plastic canopy covering some construction project.

The whole effect was an utter mystery of transparency upon transparency. Four or five layers all melting and merging into each other. Never in my life have I seen such a complex, simple, clean and playful painting. What freedom nature offers us! There is no question of what to do or what to paint. We are continuously participating in the play of nature itself.

When we reach to the height of consciousness, whatever we express shows its newness and brings a new message. We don't need to go to art school to learn techniques in order to achieve this state.

Basically, this is what I share when I teach. Free from the stories of the past, we can rejoice moment to moment as our creativity flows like the river of life itself.

Become a Midwife to Your Painting

My job is to help people to become midwives to their own paintings. In other words, I bring them into a psychological space where they are willing to let the painting give birth to itself – just helping it along. When they don't apply their ideas about where the lines should go, when they're not thinking about any particular shape or form, when they allow the mixed mediums of acrylics, inks and watercolours to find their own way on the paper, then forms appear that people have never seen or imagined.

They aren't 'doing' the painting. They're open to surprise: a strong red brush stroke curving across the paper merges with white that is not yet dry, dissolving at their borders into pink, creating a mysterious contrast to the underlying darkness of black and so on.

"Don't just do it, feel it," I suggest. "Now we are entering into a world where you are no more the host. You are the guest of the painting. And please receive the painting as a whole – don't just concentrate in the centre of the paper.

"Look at it, everywhere. Everywhere is as important as the middle. And if nothing is happening, don't collapse and start saying 'Oh, why is my painting so boring!' This is a good moment to explore. Do something new and unexpected."

We are so habituated to focus on what is missing, on what is wrong in us, on what we lack in the way of skills and talent. Through guiding people in this way, they slowly find the beauty in the painting and in themselves. People start experiencing a totally new way of painting, growing in a new direction, a new dimension, and a new wonderland.

Painting with Heart

We are coming to the end of this investigation of how art, therapy and meditation can be combined to bring more joy, harmony and vitality into our lives. So, I would like to leave you with an exercise you can do anywhere, at any time, which will remind you of your capacity to transform all kinds of situations that we meet in daily life. It's a telegraphic message without words, helping people become more connected to their own sense of beauty.

As an example, imagine that you are a participant in one of my workshops or trainings, looking at other people's paintings, and you find yourself standing in front of one that you don't particularly like.

Then you receive an invitation from me saying, "Imagine that you can bring your own painting here and merge it with some beautiful aspect of this painting. What kind of painting will it become?"

Something incredibly important can happen in moments like these. As a participant, when you stand before this painting, imagining your painting merging with it, you are painting in your heart. Nothing is happening on the outside, but the painting is happening inside, in your private inner space.

This simple exercise helps people become part of this beautiful existence, because through it you can keep on painting, anytime, anywhere, without paints, paper and brushes. You have the power to bring your heart into any situation, transforming it with love and creativity.

Who cares about material painting? What is really important is your own energy and your way of looking at life. You can participate in the creativity of nature in any moment, at any time. You are creating, each moment, without doing anything.

Appendix

Meera's long-time assistants share a few words about their experiences during her courses to illustrate Meera's unorthodox ways of guiding them, and her readiness to challenge them at any moment.

The anecdotes and insights have been chosen arbitrarily and do not constitute any form of evaluation; many others could have been added by those who were, and still are, part of her caravan of creativity.

Self-acceptance

After having worked with Meera as an assistant, I decided to take part in a self-portrait course as a participant. I wanted to work on an issue I had with my eyes that had started since childhood. I have a lazy eye that does not align with the other and I had problems painting them. Meera told me not to focus on that and make a big story out of it.

I dived fully into the group experience and on the last day, when we were asked to share whatever we had gone through, I suddenly realised that there was no longer an issue around painting my eyes, no thoughts, no memories. I had just painted them. This was a major breakthrough for me – a self-acceptance and appreciation of the unique quality of my eyes; my unique trees and my life in general. I realised once again that Meera had created a process of transformation that was much more than painting.

Ojas

"Creativity needs commitment"

For years, Meera had been waiting for some red flowers to blossom on her balcony, and they finally did during the busiest time of the training. So, she said, "Okay, if you are blossoming now, I say 'yes' to what is happening and will paint you while you flower." She set her alarm clock for 6 o'clock in the morning and painted them for an hour each morning before coming to the training. She often said that creativity needs commitment.

Nirvi

The *sakura* tree

During our *sakura* cherry blossom training in Japan one night, Meera didn't come back from painting and dinner was almost over, so I went to check on her. There she was under a beautiful *sakura* tree, totally immersed into her painting. It was cold and dark, except for the little light that illuminated the tree, and she hadn't eaten anything. I reluctantly interrupted her by asking if she wanted to come and eat. She said that she preferred to be alone, so I left.

I am lucky that she shared her passion for creativity so generously with us, although I could see that she could have been satisfied to paint alone, like most other artists do. She always said that painting is not as important as working with people. It was igniting the passion for creativity in others' hearts and sharing her love for meditation that really fulfilled her.

Chandra

Painting: a mirror of my inner world

I attended my first training with Meera with no expectation, just for pleasure. "I am not here to entertain nor to help you make a decorative painting. Art is a bridge to life. That's what I do," she said.

What a shock! Already on my first day I was in tears and fell apart. All my beliefs and old patterns were shattered. I had been studying art and painting for a long time, but had never found an intimate connection with what I was doing until then. My old way of expressing myself was like a mask, something constructed through ideas.

Now painting became a mirror of my inner world. Everything I was hiding was exposed and I started to show my real self.

Sahaja

Painting in a group

When we paint together on one large piece of paper as a group, we learn not just to be playful and innocent like a child, but also to become conscious of our way of relating. Our inner world is reflected on the canvas in front of us. Do I respect or violate mine or others' boundaries? Can I melt with others or do I isolate myself? Am I pleasing and forget my own needs, or do I overpower others? Meera used painting as a powerful tool to develop awareness in us and, in this exercise, we had the opportunity to continuously inquire about ourselves.

Sahaja

She paints what she can't see"

It was the last day of Nature Painting and Meera was showing to the group the trees we had painted. When mine was being shown, I remember her looking at me, straight into the eyes, then turned to the group and said, "She paints what she can't see."

That night I went to bed in a state of confusion, with that sentence ringing in my ears, and asked myself, "What the hell does she mean?" I felt that Meera was pointing to where I needed to look, but in that moment, I just couldn't see it.

Once back home, I hung my painting on the wall in the living room and each time I passed by, I looked at this big tree that I had painted, with its big strong roots going into the earth, hearing Meera's words, "She paints what she can't see." More than a year later I finally got it! Meera was right. I had painted those big roots, but I couldn't see them in me.

My father had died only four months before and I needed to get in touch with him. I realised he was the one who had given me those big, strong roots. It was not only about recognising that my parents were my roots, but about feeling the connection with them, acknowledging what I had received from them and honouring those gifts.

Meera used to say that paintings never lie, "Whoever you are, whatever you are feeling in the moment will find its expression on the paper and reflect back to you who you are."

Sonia

The big tree

One day I was painting plants and leaves on the lower part of my painting. Meera came along and said to me, "Vijan, you are just decorating your painting. We don't do that here. Why don't you paint a big tree?" I did not really feel like painting a tree in that moment. I resisted her advice for a while, but finally started to paint a big black tree in the middle of my painting, from bottom to top. Then I realised that the harmony and the beauty had disappeared. I tried to fix it, but nothing worked. I was shocked and started crying because I had lost my beautiful painting.

I was sad for two days and even became angry with her. Eventually I understood that it was me who was at fault. Meera had just challenged me and my attachment to preserve what I saw as beautiful, rather than moving with my energy and taking risks. I had followed her advice literally rather than taking her comment as a wake-up call and discover my own inner impulses. By not listening to my inner voice and just doing what she suggested I lost the connection with my creative drive.

Vijan

Spontaneity and discipline

People often mention Meera's spontaneity, but she was also very disciplined. For instance, for the groups she would always have the right music and quotes ready for the theme of the day. She often spoke about spontaneity and discipline as one of her life koans.

Nirvi

"Trust yourself more"

I was finishing a big cherry blossom painting but was not happy with it and became very tense. The painter next to me said that an interesting flow has been lost. I thought so too and asked a young Taiwanese friend, who I considered as very good, what he did when he got stuck. He said he would destroy the painting and start afresh.

Even though we had less than an hour left, I threw yellow colour on the painting and wiped the whole surface with it – it turned orangish. Meera had often emphasised the importance of not being attached to what we have created and that it is the process that is important, not the result. I felt good that I had the courage to take a risk even if I lost the whole painting.

However, when Meera saw the painting she let out a shout and asked why I had done that. After I told her about the feedback I got and the advice from the young friend, she said with sadness, "You have to trust yourself more." It penetrated me deeply.

A couple of months later I brought up the incident and reminded her of the painting I had made. All of a sudden, she slapped me on the cheek, though very gently, saying, "What you did to your painting!" It was as soft and loving a slap as I could ever imagine. But this taught me once again how deeply she knew of the importance of trusting and valuing oneself.

Tosho

"Life is wild"

Meera's painting class had many artists as participants. I, however had never painted before and was struggling. The artist next to me had painted a beautiful lotus flower; it was just perfect. She happily sat before her picture and waited for new instructions.

Meera came over and asked her to continue with her painting, but the artist said, "I don't know what else to do, it is finished." Meera asked her to close her eyes, took a big brush with black paint and made a big black splash on the picture. "Now open your eyes," she said to the participant. The artist had tears in her eyes – her painting was destroyed!

"This is what life is," Meera explained, "it is never finished. It is wild and unexpected. Go with it. Continue."

I was shocked about Meera's wildness. Her way of conveying a message was frightening. What to say about the wild content of the message!

Samarpan

Zen hits

Sometimes we were a bit afraid of Meera because she could be very direct and say things in a sharp way.

When she was asked, "How can you be so direct with the participants? Aren't you afraid to hurt people by being so honest?" she replied, "I am never so direct if I do not feel love. I always check with myself whether I am coming from my heart or not. That is very important, because if there is no love, my words will not reach people. But if there is love, people can resonate with something deep inside their heart."

I was touched when I heard this, and it gave me a deep understanding of how to work with people.

Kantu

Effortlessness of meditation

When I first met Meera it was during the launch of a big exhibition of her paintings. I was thoroughly impressed to see her beautiful paintings; they were so unlike paintings of modern art. Meera's were so different – painted with a deep love for nature and beauty and with the effortlessness of meditation.

Shrira

The beauty of brown

I was assisting Meera in Miasto and we were in the middle of 'the mud of Primal Painting'; maybe it was extra muddy and brown in Italy, with these earthy impulsive Italians. We were throwing onto the paper many different coloured paints which then inevitably turned into an ugly brown muddy mass. I had such a resistance against both the muddy colours and the abstract forms we had to paint.

Before taking the train back to Denmark Meera confronted me saying, "Nirvi, there is a psychological block, a fear to see yourself," and asked me to continue painting forms as an exercise at home. The next time I was with her again I painted a long vertical watercolour painting only with brown colours and she commented, "Nirvi is discovering the beauty of the brown colour."

Meera had a way of confronting us with the truth that was not always very comfortable, but what I have received from being with her is seeing her unique qualities and saying 'yes' to life with totality.

Nirvi

A hard hit

After Meera had pointed out my unawareness because I had taken another person's shoes by mistake, I started to point out what I considered her own unawareness. After another childish provocative remark of mine, during group-sharing time, she turned towards me and with piercing eyes gave me a hard hit. For what seemed like a long time she kept repeating how my meditativeness was false and borrowed. I felt destroyed and went into a state of shock. I could not make sense of what she had said and what she thought I had done to deserve such a hard hit.

After many hours of self-reflection, I started to get deeper insights about myself, about Meera and her work with us; the work we did with her was not about painting or therapy, but about learning to be in the moment without having any future goals. I started to see that the desire to create something beautiful is the reason for frustration. I also understood that Meera had been trying to show us something that cannot be put into words.

When I met Meera two days later she asked, "Did I give you a hard time?" I nodded. "I don't know why I said these things; they were out of context, weren't they?" I nodded again. "This was the first time I addressed your mind, because normally I picture you as a no-mind painter." Still nodding I shared all what I had gone through. She smiled and said that she was very happy that I understood what her work was all about.

Premraj

Meera, the typhoon

We helpers usually had the painting material ready for the day according to a plan, but Meera often changed her mind and asked us to prepare totally different materials, right before the start of the workshop. We would run around here and there like ants, trying to get everything ready according to the new plan. She never took in consideration if it was difficult for us or not – all we could do was to go along and ride on her energy wave.

Working with Meera was like being in a huge typhoon. It was an inspiration for me that another Japanese woman, like me, was daring enough to behave like this, even at the risk of annoying others.

One day, Meera told me, "I am sorry if I behave like this, but I need to follow my intuition and trust each moment where my energy is taking me."

Kantu

The artist's ego

Many years ago, there was a period when I was having a hard time with Meera. Whatever I said or did, she never said 'yes' to me. I felt hurt and rejected and couldn't understand why. At one time she told me, "It is not me who is speaking. Something is speaking through me."

Only later did I realise that my ego as an artist was resisting her. When I got the point, the feeling of love and intimacy returned, and I understood that when there is love one can also be hard. Only because I always felt this love in her trainings was I able to stay on, even in those difficult moments.

Bhaven

A big gift

After six years of having been a staff member, I got a shock when I was told in front of the entire group that next year I should come as a participant. I felt excluded from the team I had been part of for so long and asked myself what I might have done wrong.

The following year I arrived as a participant, and when Meera hugged me I could feel I was holding back, still frozen from that shock. The first day my attention was focused on the helper team; watching them do the job I had done for so many years, until I became aware that my energy was turned outwards whilst I needed it for myself.

While being a helper, Meera had asked me many times whether I enjoyed painting because I was more focused on taking care of the participants. As a result, I was painting mechanically. I was not fully connected with myself. I had forgotten how to be wild, how to dance and enjoy painting!

Meera had seen what was going on with me, how much I was missing, and gave me this *big* gift by asking me to come as a participant!

Anando

Two paintings become one

Once in the Nature Painting part of a training Meera suggested I should get my primal painting and put it side by side to the nature painting. I did not understand what she had in mind. Only days later, when I was struggling to complete my nature painting, I understood. Suddenly an unexpected turn happened and I saw these two paintings become one.

Bhaven

Just a few splashes and strokes – so beautiful

Meera was demonstrating a simple procedure, painting in tandem with a partner. The partner sitting behind you moves your hand that holds the brush. You do not see what he is painting because you have your eyes closed. Once in a while he says, "Open your eyes," immediately followed by, "Close your eyes."

Meera did the demonstration with me. I closed my eyes and she started to splash colours using my hand. After a few splashes she said, "Open your eyes," and what I saw was so beautiful that tears came to my eyes. Just a few splashes and strokes and what was in front of my eyes was so stunningly beautiful.

Tosho

"You have become an Italian"

In difficult times I always remember what Meera once told me: "Be simple!" It immediately helps me come down to earth and out of my mind. She showed me through her way of living that life is a dance, a dance of opposites and that things keep on changing and moving all the time. That is why there is no finished painting really. One can always continue, just as life knows no full stop. She taught me to live the big adventure of life with an open heart without holding on to anything.

One day in Nature Painting Meera came to me, looked at my work, smiled and said, "Now, Sahaja, you have really learned to be an Italian!"

Sahaja

Breaking the piggy-bank

Towards the end of a long training participants usually try to finish their paintings. We were carefully making touch-ups here and there, when Meera said to the group while passing by a few of us, "That's an instalment saving! How about breaking open your piggy bank? You could find a 10,000 yen note there. Break it open!"

"What is she talking about? I might just find 0 yen inside!" I thought to myself.

A few people were courageous enough to break open their piggy bank and changed their paintings dramatically. But I couldn't find that much courage and kept following the patterns I had already painted.

Meera came to me and said, "Your painting will turn out like one by a middle-aged auntie!" I laughed and was impressed by her accurate and humorous expression.

So, I took the jump!
Henna

"Paint what you love"

One time in Nature Painting I was somehow just going through the motions, painting mechanically, not really being in my heart. Meera saw that – because, as you may know, she saw everything – and came running towards me, took me by the hand, made me stand up and run with her around Buddha Grove.

She stopped here and there to show me the beauty that I had been blind to. Then she made me kneel by the bamboos and touch them and said, "Paint like this, paint what you love."
Swan

Emptiness and fulfilment

My boyfriend and I had just broken up and my dreams of having a family were thus shattered. I would have been ready to have a baby, with hormones at their peak as I was approaching 40. When I walked into the group room and saw a sweet, two-year old girl, I was in shock. A participant had taken along her baby including her mother to take care of the child. Of course, Meera also included the grandmother in the group, creating space for her to join and paint whenever she could.

Towards the end of the group we made a circle holding hands, and by coincidence I came to sit between Meera and the grandmother. While sitting in the circle, we looked into each other's eyes, one by one. I looked into the eyes of the grandmother and, instead of seeing a mature woman, I saw a neglected young girl longing to be seen and appreciated, hoping to finally stop nourishing others and start nourishing herself. When I turned to my left I saw a spiritual mother, who could nourish so many people with genuine compassion and never hesitate to tell the truth. Looking into Meera's eyes – for what felt like eternity – I saw fulfilment not only as a woman, but as a soul. This suddenly shifted my fixation on motherhood.

Chandra

Existential art

25 years ago, when I saw Meera's paintings exhibited in a gallery at the Osho International Meditation Resort, I had my first experience where paintings hit me so hard that electricity literally went up my spine. There was something in her paintings that was so alive, beautiful, deep and existential.

Tosho

Flexibility: beyond Japanese conditioning

Often Meera spontaneously changed what she had planned to do in the group and we as helpers often got caught by surprise having to quickly adjust and prepare new materials or spaces according to her new plan. I learned to put my mind and preferences aside and follow the new direction and flow. I also learned to be flexible and be aware of each moment. Meera's readiness to change direction any moment made the whole group process alive and full of surprises. I started feeling excited like a child never knowing what would happen next. Only this moment is important!

Contrary to my Japanese conditioning I started to develop the trust that I will be able to deal with whatever happens next. Rather than coming from fear and the safety of following a pre-conceived plan, I learned that true creativity arises only out of such moments of not knowing. Wanting perfection kills creativity. Meera demonstrated how to respond with flexibility and joy to unexpected events and circumstances in life.

Tathina

"You don't have to cry"

During Nature Painting I got stuck because there were too many leaves in the trees! Especially in India nature is so abundant, with such huge trees that I was simply overwhelmed. Looking up at the sky, I cried out helplessly. I was wailing when Meera approached me and said, "You don't have to cry."

Something clicked in me and I became aware of my tendency to be perfect. After that I was able to paint the abundance of nature without any effort.

Fulwari

Relax into nature

"I am still trying, Meera," I said after a morning of sitting in the bushes struggling to capture the light of a small leaf I was painting.

"You are judging yourself." She looked at me.

"It's so hard, the light keeps changing," I replied.

"It's your idea that light should shine in one direction. How can you ask the sun to stay fixed in one place in the sky?" she said, raising her hands high up into the sky. "Remember, we have to be humble in front of nature. Nature does not judge. Relax! Relax into nature," and held her hands wide open and smiled.

Dariya

Darkness and light

I loved to look at the stems of the bamboos in the golden afternoon light. As much as I loved them, I struggled to get the feeling of the shining light onto my paper. Suddenly I felt a light hand on my left shoulder and heard Meera's voice, "I see that painting is your love. What are you looking for?"

"The light," I replied.

"I see," she said and took my brush, mixed an almost black colour and painted two strokes next to a yellow stem. Now the shining light of the bamboos started to show, so easily and naturally.

She then added, "If you want to have light, don't avoid darkness!"

Jheel

"Nothing will ever be the same"

One morning while painting in Buddha Grove as usual – I don't exactly remember what triggered this – I saw the futility of my struggle to do it 'right'.

It was a moment of clarity and I realised that life, and Osho, were giving me so much that it was up to me to open up and receive it. A clear image appeared in my mind: I was in the ocean, surrounded by an infinite stretch of water, but there I was still holding onto my small water bottle. I felt overwhelmed, as if my heart could no longer fit in my chest, and walked over to Meera who was standing at the DJ's desk where she was preparing the music for a dance interval. She saw me crying and immediately understood that these were tears of gratitude, not of misery. She hugged me and said, "Once you cry like this, nothing will ever be the same."

When I went back to my painting, I enjoyed playing with colours on the paper, without a goal. I now understood what Meera meant when she said, "It doesn't matter if you do this stroke or that stroke. If you enjoy the process it will show in your painting."

Chandra

Abundance: "This is our style!"

Meera used to invite all helpers and assistants – we were usually at least ten of us – to the breakfast buffet of a nearby 5-star hotel. Everyone was touched by her generosity. Once Meera said, "Okay, so this is our style! Enjoy the abundance inside and outside!" Those simple words gave me a big relief and confirmation that it is okay to enjoy life in any situation.

Kantu

Only after facing the dark side can we express beauty

In the workshops Meera also included therapy work. It was clear to her that, on the way to beauty and truth, we had to face the dark side and accept where we come from with totality, embrace our parents and all events that happened in our lives. Only after being confronted with many deep wounds and painful memories can we come to our true nature and express something of beauty.

Shrira

The art to be total

Meera taught me what unconditional love is and the art of being total, to be joyful every moment like an innocent child who sees everything for the first time. In our 25 years of being together she kept surprising me and fall in love with her again and again.

I wish that her paintings continue to bring a glimpse of happiness and silence into the hearts of those who look at them and that the work she initiated will continue to flower and bear new fruits. Thank you, beloved, for having been my fellow traveller in this life, for still showing me the beauty of life and for touching my heart endlessly.

Svagito

About the Author

Meera (Kazue Hashimoto) started painting in early childhood. Born in a small fisherman's village in Ishikawa, Japan in 1947, she studied Japanese Dance and Art at Tokyo University. In her twenties she travelled via Russia to Europe visiting the famous art museums and eventually settled in Toledo, Spain, where she continued to study and practise art. In Toledo, where she lived for seven years, she became a founding member of a famous art group, the Grupo Tolmo, that exhibited all over Spain.

When, in 1974, she met the enlightened Master Osho in India, and became his disciple, her way of painting and her vision of creativity changed drastically.

In Osho's vision true creativity does not come from the mind or intellectual concepts, as in conceptual art for example, but is born from an inner space of silence. Art understood in this way becomes an outer expression of the inner beauty that we discover in a state of meditation.

In 1976 Osho asked Meera to create the Rajneesh Art School (later Osho Art School) and she started leading art workshops and trainings around the world, which she continued till her last course in January 2017.

Many of Meera's paintings are inspired by Osho's discourses and she regularly showed them to Osho, who commented on her work and helped her to expand her vision of creativity. He personally chose many of her paintings to illustrate more than 40 publications of his books.

Besides working at the Osho Resort in Pune, India, Meera also created art communities in Italy, the Netherlands and Belgium and held art exhibitions in galleries around the world.

In her work with people she was not focused on teaching any painting technique, but rather help the participants to discover their authentic creative impulse and unique expression.

She developed new ways to use painting as a method for inner transformation. In her courses and trainings, that are also documented on various DVDs, she integrated many therapeutic methods, including Star Sapphire energy work, Family Constellation and dance therapy. As she once said, "I am having two legs, on one I am a painter and on the other, I am a therapist."

The rare combination of being an unconventional artist and at the same a meditator, filled with compassion for people and their inner growth, made her courses and training groups a life-changing experience for many.

Meera died in a scuba-diving accident in South Africa on 21st February 2017.

Meera Art Foundation

The Meera Art Foundation, the publisher of this book, has been created by Meera's husband, Svagito. Its goal is to preserve Meera's art and her life's work and to make them available to a larger public, and support artists who work in the field of meditative art. Meera's books, her DVDs and prints of her paintings are available through the Foundation's website.

With gratitude to all those who contributed to create the Foundation and are working to keep Meera's vision and work alive. Thank you to Jheel who manages the Foundation and helped in establishing it, to Hamido who created the cover of this book and all of Meera's DVDs; to Premendra who photographed Meera's paintings and takes care of the archive; to Angela who created our amazing website; to the Osho Miasto team who is at the forefront of helping us create a museum to exhibit Meera's artwork, and to all helpers and assistants who keep supporting our projects and exhibitions so generously.

Anyone who wishes to contribute and support the continuation of Meera's work, please contact the Meera Art Foundation:

www.meera-art-foundation.com

Books by Meera

ReAwakening of Art: A radical new look at how creativity is born (Perfect Publishers 2005)

Blossoming: (art book by Meera and Satyam, only available through Meera Art Foundation)

Watch Meera online: vimeo.com/ondemand/artmeera

www.ingramcontent.com/pod-product-compliance
Lightning Source LLC
Chambersburg PA
CBHW030925180526
45163CB00002B/470